If The Story Fits, Tell It

REGINA STONE MATTHEWS

No part of this book may be reproduced or transmitted in any form or by any means electronic or mechanical, including photocopying and recording, or by any information storage or retrieval systems, without permission in writing from the author. The only exception is by a reviewer, who may quote short excerpts in a review.

Copyright © 2020 by Regina Stone Matthews
All rights reserved.
www.reginamatthews.com
Atwater & Bradley Publishers

ISBN: 978-1-7332127-6-2

All Scripture quotations, unless otherwise indicated are taken from the Holy Bible, New International Version®, NIV® Copyright ©1973, 1978, 1984, 2011 by Biblica, Inc.® Used by permission. All rights reserved worldwide.

For the storyteller in everyone.

May the stories you tell spark the imagination of your listeners.

May you live out your dream of telling stories.

To all my storytelling friends who taught me not only the art of storytelling but the joy of it as well.

Contents

A Note to Readers vii
Preface ix
Introduction xiii
The Magic of Storytelling xiii
Part 1: Different Types of Storytelling 1
Part 2: What's the Deal About the Hook? 9
Part 3: The Myths and Truths of Storytelling 12
Part 4: Structure of a Story and Parts of a Story 14
Part 5: The Story Spine 19
Part 6: Body Movement and Voice Inflection 21
Part 7: More About Storytelling 23
Part 8: The Greatest Storyteller of All Time: Jesus 25
Story #1: A Girl Can Never Wear Too Much Blue Eye Shadow 31
Story #2: Basic Needs 39
Story #3: Dear Dishwasher 45
Story #4: Death Can Really Ruin Your Day 51
Story #5: Does Anyone Really Know Polk Salad Annie? 59
Story #6: Don't Try to Perm Your Own Hair & Never Wear High-Heels on a Soggy Lawn 65
Story #7: Dreamin' big and Livin' large 71
Story #8: Elizabeth Marie Hutchinson: The Character Behind the Character 77

Story #9: Happy Birthday Sweet Sixteen 83

Story #10: If It's Not One Thing It's Your Mother 89

Story #11: Imperfections 95

Story #12: Marcia Brady…Women's Libber! 101

Story #13: Mothers, Daughters, High Heels, and Pearls 109

Story #14: Mr. Wolf 117

Story #15: My Mother's Hands 123

Story #16: Pardon Me, But I Think I've Lost My Way to Sesame Street 129

Story #17: The Difference Between Peggy and Aunt Virginia . 135

Story #18: Redneckness Must Be a Disease 143

Story #19: Superfluous Buns 149

Story #20: The Corncob Pipe in Daddy's Pipe Stand 155

Story #21: The Day the Handshake Died 161

Story #22: There Ain't Enough Rice to Cover Up the Catfish!. 167

Story #23: The Unmasking of the Masks 175

Story #24: Third Grade 181

Story #25: What's It All About If It Ain't About the Bling? 187

Also by Regina Stone Matthews 196

A Note to Readers

I'M SO PLEASED THAT STORYTELLING IS MAKING A COMEBACK IN A huge way. I hope that if you are considering storytelling as a hobby or even as a career that this book will whet your appetite enough to give you that push toward storytelling.

Certainly, there are many instructional books available for storytellers. They offer in-depth teachings and some even get into the weeds of storytelling. This book, however, gives the beginning storyteller an idea of what storytelling is all about. It's an intro into the world of storytelling. I guarantee it won't make your head hurt.

At the end of the instruction sections, I've provided you with twenty-five stories that are great for storytelling. Keep in mind that these are stand-alone stories. They read as such and should not be confused with one continuous story. These are stories I've told that I know you'll enjoy. They range from humorous to tissue worthy, but they all carry with them personal experiences and my heart.

I love writing short stories and have written two books of short stories—one a Christian Literary Award winner. Storytelling in every form starts out on paper. For oral storytellers, we take that written story and put a spin to it using the techniques you'll find in this book. And because telling a good story requires developing a good storyline, I'll discuss that, too.

I'm so proud to be a part of your learning experience and hope at the end of this book you'll have decided to learn more about the art of storytelling.

Preface

Before humans could write, storytelling existed through the spoken word. I've been in love with storytelling my entire life. As a short story and children's book author, stories are my passion. There's no doubt in my mind that I could sit for hours listening to people tell stories.

As a youngster, I made up stories and acted them out in plays that I put on at my house on the front porch. My parents encouraged my imagination and storytelling by allowing me to host plays on Saturday afternoons. Mother made me a curtain that my daddy hung over a rope he tied between two of the pillars on our porch. My afternoon plays were a big hit in the neighborhood. When asked why I didn't charge for my shows I remember saying that I just couldn't find it in my heart to make people pay to watch me do something I loved to do. I simply wanted them to have a good time. Thus began my life of make-believe.

Storytelling can inform, educate, and entertain. The earliest storytellers were influential and respected in their cultures. Long before Christ, people of means hired storytellers to tell stories to their families.

My mother took great joy in introducing me to fairy tales, and I came to love them as much as she did. Even before I learned to read, she would act out the story as she read it to me.

The evolution of storytelling—from the beginning of time until now—can boggle the mind. And although the methods by which we seek out stories have changed drastically over the years, it's still interesting to dig into the wonderment of storytelling in all its forms.

Coming from a Native American background, the story of the Thunderbird always thrilled and amazed me. To explain thunder and lightning, storytellers told of an enormously powerful and magical bird. His wings flapped with such intensity that they caused thunder in the clouds. When he became angry, lightning would shoot out of his eyes. The Thunderbird's power could be both good and bad—he brought the rain, but also the storms. The story of the medicine bear is another one of those stories I grew to respect. It's a little scary but carries with it a memorable lesson. This is a story that requires great listening skills. But, then, that's the point. A good storyteller beckons one to listen.

I'm so delighted and honored to share a little of the historical background, styles, and types of storytelling. Then we'll get into those stories I mentioned previously.

It's going to be a fun ride!

If the Story Fits, Tell It

Introduction

The Magic of Storytelling

Whether in written storytelling or oral storytelling, the key objective for any storyteller is to captivate the audience. To find the magic in the story. When a storyteller is able to connect with an audience, the power of the story carries the audience to another moment in time, another world, be it familiar or foreign. This is what I love about telling stories. They have the power to transform.

Once upon a time, I met a lady who invited me to a storyteller's guild meeting. At the time I had no idea what a guild like this had to offer. I knew I loved to listen to stories so I thought it certainly couldn't hurt to go take a look. At the end of the guild meeting, I could hardly contain my enthusiasm. I knew I must join. And so I did. I've now been a member of the North 40 Storytellers Guild for a little over nine years. To say I've enjoyed every minute of it is an understatement. Not to mention how much I've learned over the years.

It's not easy to get up in front of a group of people to tell a story. It's especially daunting to tell a story in front of a group of professionally seasoned storytellers for the first time. Talk about nerves. But regardless of nerves, I consider joining a storyteller's guild as a must.

Over the past several years I've had the pleasure of telling at a few events. I also had the honor of representing my guild as their rising star at the Tejas Storytelling Association Annual Festival. I've also told holiday stories, scary stories, murder and mayhem stories, and special event stories over the years. So many different venues provide a terrific platform for storytellers.

The goal of any story is to get the listener to say, "Tell me more about that." As the author of your story, begin by deliberately writing out your story with conviction and purpose. Remember, you must make an emotional connection with your audience to make the story stick.

So, what's your story?

Does it ignite the inner fire of your audience? Strive to educate them? Always try to motivate your audience. If you are bold and don't mind getting pushback, you might want to consider stories that perpetuate a movement. No matter the goal or subject of your story, make it simple, not complicated. Complicated stories put your audience to sleep.

If you are the competitive type, there are all sorts of storytelling competitions. One that fascinates me is The Moth, a non-profit group who sponsor theme-based events across the U.S. The themes are usually posted at the beginning of the season so that tellers can tell a story based on the theme they like best. Then the tellers participate in a StorySLAM in front of judges. Winners move on to the GrandSLAM. The catch is, the storytellers also known as "slammers" have only five minutes each to tell the theme-based story. Pretty cool!

Then there's Fringe Theatre which is simply productions that are experimental either in subject matter or style. They are usually very interesting. Fringe is not for the weak at heart as it can prod and poke many emotions.

Oral storytelling is an art that involves focusing on many

pieces at once. The teller must be aware of facial expressions and tone of voice, which can advance a story. One's body language is particularly important. Gestures always add to the story. How the teller affixes his eyes is important, too. Oral storytellers should always take into consideration the space around them, make sure they face the audience, and don't turn away from them.

I've never regretted my first visit to my storyteller's guild. It opened my mind to a craft I've loved since childhood. I'll be forever grateful to all those storytellers who have shared their talent and their knowledge with me.

Part 1

Different Types of Storytelling

Folktales

If you love stories that have been passed down from generation to generation, you'll love folktales. Generally, folktales are oral stories, meaning they came to us from an era when literacy did not exist. While folktales are passed down, each person will add some new little bit, something more interesting or exciting or fascinating. Consequently, what might have started out as fact can easily turn to fiction. Keep in mind that there are some folktales that stay intact making the folktale nonfiction. Each folktale forms alongside the culture or customs of the particular village or country from which the story originated. These stories come from all over the world, but are extremely prevalent in Africa or Australia or Asia. There are also several European folktales, too.

Fairy Tales

Who doesn't love fairy tales? My favorite, for sure. Enchanted forests, unicorns, talking animals, elves, fairies. Magic kingdoms with dragons and trolls and ogres. There are lots of princesses and princes in fairy tales. Along with kings and queens. All the usual characters and places.

Although fairy tales are a part of folklore, they tend to take on a magic of their own. They usually take place *once upon a time,* and are generally filled with happiness and romance. Goodness always wins which for me is such a hook. I love happy endings, and fairy tales often offer that. At least that is how we identify them now. One fun fact I learned is that fairy tales in their original forms could be quite gruesome. When they were reproduced for a wider, more literate audience, the violence was toned down so the listener or reader could better relate to the story.

Fables

Fables fall into their own literary genre. They are fictional. Fables take many forms in their telling. They can revolve around people, inanimate objects, or animals, plants, and even insects. But no matter the character, they always have a moral, a lesson to be taught from the story.

We've all heard of *Aesop's Fables*. One I particularly remember is *The Ant and the Grasshopper,* which teaches us we should always work hard and plan for the future. Fables are great for telling about extraordinary people—heroes if you will.

Legends, Traditional and Urban

Legends are super cool as they can be about real people. Though they can be based in history, they often take on believability amid fiction. For instance, most of us know the legend of George Washington cutting down the cherry tree and his determination not to tell a lie. Traditional legends, such as this one, are usually old, and the people in them have most likely passed on.

Urban Legends have only been around since about 1968. Urban Legends are stories the teller relates about a friend or a family member who met with horrifying elements. It can also take a turn toward comedy through exaggeration. Although Urban Legends are mostly entertaining, they can be a bit dark since many focus on troubling events.

Pourquoi Tales

Pourquoi tales attempt to explain why things are the way they are. The why and the how. Like why tigers have stripes or snakes have no legs. There are all types of Native American stories in this genre, such as why an opossum's tail is bare or why a buffalo has a hump or even how daylight came to be are just a few. Pourquoi Tales allow the listener to connect with the culture from which it originates as well. This type of tale is so much fun to listen to. You never know what direction the teller will take the story. Pourquoi tales are also considered folktales.

Family or Personal Tales

This seems easy, right? But it isn't. Sometimes the personal tale is hurtful. Sometimes it brings back unpleasant memories. When you share a memory in the art of storytelling, it must be specific in its makeup. That's why it's difficult to tell family or personal stories. My Uncle Worth told the best stories, but he only told personal and family stories. Even if you weren't a character in the story or had never heard the story when he told it, you felt you were right there. Specifics. That was his key. Family and personal stories bind us together because we can relate to the journey of emotions.

Tall Tales

Now, this is my kind of storytelling. I love tall tales. A tall tale is a total exaggeration of an event or a person. You get to use all sorts of incredibly unbelievable elements to get your audience involved in this web of craziness. Hyperbole is the ruler of the tall tale. A tall tale can even include a few facts, but of course it is mostly fiction. When telling a tall tale, you can include yourself in the story. It's a super fun way of hooking your audience.

How did tall tales begin? Many years ago, when folks gathered and began telling oral stories, some included a little bragging about themselves. Then another teller would want to one-up the previous story and embellish his own experiences. Even some American literature incorporates a bit of the tall tale. When telling a tall tale, the teller is just as important as the story itself. Why? Because it's the teller's job to tell the tale as if it were true. Keeping the audience wondering is key.

Multicultural Tales

Easy enough. Stories that speak to different cultures. Multicultural tales reflect the culture of their subjects—Native Americans or Asian Americans or Latino Americans or African Americans or the Jews. These can be extremely educational stories, whether based on fictitious characters or places or on factual ones.

Spooky Tales

Again, easy to see this kind of storytelling. We're talking tales that scare the pants off your audience if told correctly. Spooky stories and ghost stories can be told to both adults and children. However, when choosing a spooky tale for children, the teller must be aware of his audience as it pertains to age and appropriateness of the story. Spooky tales may be any kind of drama as long as there's some sort of spirit—or the possibility of a spirit—lurking around. Magical or haunting happenings usually occur in spooky tales. The element of surprise is always good when telling spooky tales.

Telling with Props (puppets, musical instruments, misc. props)

Storytelling with props is especially helpful and fun when telling stories to children. It has a way of adding substance to the words. Even if you're telling a story to adults, using props, or playing a musical instrument can enhance your story. Another thing about props from the storyteller's point of view is that they can act as a trigger to move the story along in the correct sequence. Using props is never a bad thing to do. Just make sure your props go with your story and try to use them creatively.

Holiday Tales

Holiday tales are just that—tales about holidays. In America, we start the holiday season in October with Halloween. After that comes Thanksgiving and then Christmas. There are certainly many other holidays storytellers can use to create a story.

Holiday tales can be fiction or non-fiction. They can be about the teller or the teller's family. Family traditions surrounding any holiday always makes for a good story. You can even tell a story about a famous person and a significant holiday in their history. Holiday tales are always fun to tell.

Sacred or Historical Tales

Sacred tales are defined by their element of deep spiritual truth. Sacred tales can be developed from the Bible or other religious texts. Sacred tales often deal with the *big questions* of life. Some sacred tales are even passed down from generation to generation. More often than not, sacred tales are extremely powerful.

When telling historical tales, it's incumbent upon the teller not to mix history with fiction. It's certainly okay to tell a fictional story based on history, but historical tales should be accurate.

Myths

Myths are like sacred tales in that they speak about the world and encompass man's experiences in it. They aren't typically cheery or happily ever after, like fairy tales. They can, however, be fiction and non-fiction.

There are many definitions of a myth. A lot of myths involve a pantheon—a variety of different types—of gods and goddesses. Myths can also be about super or supernatural humans. Myths can be ancient stories passed down through the ages. A myth can also be a story about why the world is the way we see it.

One of the key elements in myths, and even folktales, is what we call the monomyth. In other words, the hero's journey throughout the story. The hero in the story finds that he must leave home and go on some journey, leaving a place he's comfortable in—a place he knows. Then the hero finds himself in an unknown place. Obviously, for the story to be interesting, the journey must be difficult. After he goes through turmoil and defeats whatever force has been against him, it's time to return home. But! He doesn't go home empty-handed. He returns with either some newfound wisdom or an actual reward. Because he's a hero, this something is not only for himself, it's something to benefit the town or village or community in which he lives. He has this need to share. And why wouldn't he? He's a hero!

Potpourri Tales

No, I'm not talking about the smelly leaves and flowers type of potpourri. In storytelling, potpourri tales are simply a collection of stories that have been put forth by the masters of storytelling. It's a total array of all sorts of stories. I love potpourri tales because you can go in any direction with your story.

Liars Tales and Competitions

The best compliment a liar's competition contestant can hear is, "You are such a liar!" Music to the ears. How do you get that compliment? Begin your story or your lie with something believable. Something that sounds like it *could* be true or *could* have happened. But it's got to sound honest. Then you start adding exaggerations into the story. The elements gradually get bigger and bigger and bigger until the audience doesn't know if they want to believe it or not. So you sprinkle a little believability into the story and then they really start to fall for what you're saying. You begin to lull the audience into getting them comfortable with you, making them laugh along the way.

As the audience starts to accept your story, you might see them nodding to one another like what you're saying is true. Now you've got them. You can go either way here. You can keep with your exaggerated story that seems believable but is a total lie or you can veer off into the world of fantasy ending your story with that "gotcha"! This is where the audience realizes you've been telling a lie the entire time. So have fun with this type of oral storytelling. Just don't fall into the pit of believing your own lies.

Part 2

What's the Deal About the Hook?

Sounds fishy to me. How about you? If your story doesn't have one, it could smell fishy. When developing a story, the teller must seriously consider the hook. Otherwise, critics might say the story stinks.

The hook of a story is just that—something that catches your audience and allows you to reel them in. The best reward for a storyteller is looking out over his audience and seeing them lean toward him. That's the sign the story has a strong opening hook.

When listening to a storyteller I want to be captivated. Oral storytelling can have a strange hold on an audience. The hook grabs the listener and pulls them into the story. That's one of the things I love about oral storytelling—inviting the audience into the story. The hook is a great way to do just that. Depending on the age of your audience and the type of story, your hook should be generationally appropriate.

Not creating a great hook can cost the teller up to 90% of his audience. The best way to get the audience to stay with you until the end of your story is the hook, which leads to the hold and ends with the payoff.

What does a good hook look like? Using words like *imagine* will aid in pulling your audience into your story. Words like *what if...* will perk the ears of your audience. Phrase your hook in such a way that it satisfies the audience's main want—make me care. You want them to care about the story you're getting ready to tell them. Masters of storytelling have the ability to make their audiences work for the story without the audience even knowing it.

We're taught in writing classes that there are at least six types of hooks.

1. Quotation Hook: Quote a famous person or anyone, really. The same goes for oral storytelling.
2. Metaphor or Simile Hook: A metaphor is a figure of speech comparing one thing to another. A simile is kinda the same except you use the words *like* or *as* before the comparison. If you use this type of hook, you force your readers to look at the topic you're writing about differently. You can do this in oral storytelling as well.
3. Interesting Question Hook: Ask a question that the reader can only answer by reading what follows. Tellers do this also. If the teller asks a question that's impossible for the audience to answer, the audience will be compelled to listen to discover the answer.
4. Description Hook: In writing, it's important to paint a picture for the reader through words. Seeing a scene in their minds draws the reader in. In oral storytelling, descriptive words about a person or place will draw the audience into your story.
5. Fact Hook: Hooking your reader with a fact or statistic they aren't aware of is a good way to keep them reading. The same for oral storytelling.

Throwing out an interesting fact to your audience will make them want to know more.
6. Declaration Hook: Strong statements, one which cause the reader to flinch or makes them want to know why and how you could make that statement is another way to hook them. This is a good hook for oral storytelling as well since it often causes your audience to sit up straight in their chairs and listen hard.

As you can see, hooks do make a difference. Used correctly, they create an interesting story. So grab hold of that hook!

Yikes!

Part 3

The Myths and Truths of Storytelling

Some myths about storytelling can sometimes dissuade a person from trying to tell their story.

Myth #1: Storytelling is not for everyone.

Truth: Storytelling *is* for everyone.

Myth #2: Storytelling cannot be used in business or professional settings.

Truth: Storytelling *can* be used very effectively in business.

Myth #3: You can't tell a story if you aren't a professional storyteller.

Truth: You absolutely can tell a story even if you are not a professional storyteller!

Myth #4: Storytellers don't write their own stories.

Truth: Storytellers can and do write their own stories. They can also (with permission from the author) retell stories that are published works.

Myth #5: Storytellers are born with the ability to tell stories.

Truth: Yes, some are born with this ability. However, storytelling is also a skill like any other profession or hobby. It can be learned and developed.

Part 4

Structure of a Story and Parts of a Story

Stories create interest. Stories get traction. Stories make us feel good. Plus, good stories have structure.

Structure

Start—The why of your story—making sure your story is about something and why it is important to tell the story.

Middle—The how of your story—the happenings of the story and how they play out.

End—The what of your story—what is the end result of the story and what did the characters do to find the resolution.

Always put your story down on paper first. Use your story to strike an emotional connection with your audience. Look at the structure of your story like you'd look at a building. Your foundation of the story is the plot. The plot needs to be strong like the foundation of a building. If there's too many cracks it will fall. Remember your characters and your setting. They represent the walls and the beams of your building. Conflict occurs when you can't decide on the type of roof or the color of the paint or even what kind of siding to use. Eventually you resolve this conflict and the building or the story is complete.

Looking at three types of stories:

The Rockstar or Hero story—a challenge is given; a challenge is rejected; a challenge is finally embraced; the world is saved.

The Maverick or Change the World story—the dreamers; the difference makers; the rule-breakers; the world is changed.

The Sherlock or Problem/Solution story—the problem is presented; the solution is determined; each concept is a character.

Parts of a Story

When I started learning about storytelling, I learned about the 5Cs of storytelling. Circumstance, curiosity, characters, conversations, and conflict.

CIRCUMSTANCE:

When crafting your story, it's important to lay out the circumstances. Set the scene. Give your audience vital information. You set the scene by giving the audience sensory descriptions. How does it look? What sounds occur? What smells filled the air? How does it feel? This will provide them with context about your story. The goal in storytelling is to leave your audience wanting more.

CURIOSITY:

If there is nothing to be curious about why would your audience keep listening? The storyteller can use curiosity as a hook to get the audience involved in the story.

CHARACTERS:

Interesting characters are extremely important in your storytelling. If the storyteller can use different voices for each character—all the better. Don't get me wrong. You can certainly tell a story without that ability. But either way, you must build up your character so that your audience wants to know what happens next. Of course, your audience will want to relate to at least one of the characters in your story. Characters and conversation go hand-in-hand.

CONVERSATIONS:

I love conversations between characters. Not all stories have a conversation, but when they do, it's always fun for the audience as it stimulates their imagination and makes the characters relatable.

CONFLICT:

This is the most important part of any story. Sometimes storytellers give way too much detail upfront. If you tell your story in chronological order, by the time you've reached the AH-HA moment, you'll most likely lose your audience. You can't wait too long to get to the exciting stuff. Personally, I have the attention span of an inch-worm, so if I'm in the audience and the storyteller's story is happening the way life happens (chronologically), I'm bored and cease to listen. Because of that, it's better to start in the middle, where things are exciting and much more interesting. You're literally making the middle your beginning.

Using conflict this way means the storyteller is using a method called *in medias res*. This means that you are hitting the audience at the height of your conflict. You're dropping them right in the middle of the heat of action. By doing this, you put your audience immediately on the edge of their seats and they will be more likely to stay with you throughout your story.

But here's a little warning…don't give too much of your conflict away. You want that immediate excitement but make sure you've got somewhere even more exciting to go.

As a beginning storyteller, I learned that appealing to the senses through your story will immediately engage your audience. It gets the entire brain engaged in the story. To help with this, use something called the principles of VAKO: Visual, Auditory, Kinesthetic, and Olfactory. If you incorporate these four elements in your story, you're more likely to draw your audience in and lock them down. Make sure, however, not to overdo it. Your story needs some meat—the 5Cs—to keep your audience engaged.

All of this sounds a bit like pulling on your audience's emotions, doesn't it? But a good story always makes your audience feel something—happy or sad or scared or content. It's critical for your audience to make an emotional connection with you and the story.

When crafting a story, think about what emotion you want to communicate and then provide information to support the emotion. And, remember, if there's no conflict then there's not much of a story. A storyteller's dream is for an audience to say, "Great story! Tell it again!" Using the 5 Cs and the senses will keep your audience on the edge of their seat and leave them wanting more.

Part 5

The Story Spine

How it fits in with the structure of the story

Sound painful? Not really. The story spine is just another way at looking at story structure. I learned about the story spine during a seminar I attended. It's another tool storytellers use to create a good story. The point of the story spine is to provide a model for a well-constructed story. The story spine starts at the beginning of the story with an established routine. Then an event breaks the routine. Next a middle that shows the consequences of having broken the routine. Then a climax sets up the resolution to the story in motion and the ending brings resolution. It looks a little like this:

Once upon a time_____

Every day_____

Until one day_____

Because of that_____

And then because of that_____

And then because of that_____

Until finally _____

And ever since then_____

So, the moral of the story is_____

    When acted out with several storytellers, each taking a blank to fill in, building on each other, it can be quite hilarious. This is a great tool to help you structure your story. Plus it's just plain fun!

Part 6

Body Movement and Voice Inflection

ONE OF THE FUN PARTS OF ORAL STORYTELLING IS BODY MOVEMENT. Don't let that scare you. And don't run out to the nearest dance studio to learn dance moves! Whether you realize it or not, we all use our body to communicate. Many of us wouldn't be able to talk if we couldn't use our hands. The same applies when storytelling.

In the beginning, storytellers tend to stand in one place. Motionless. Most likely because they're scared out of their minds to stand in front of a group to tell a story. The more stories you tell, the less the jitters. Consequently, movement becomes more natural.

Gestures, facial expressions, hand and feet movement, and especially eye contact all become a part of the story. Even the teller's attire can feed into the story, depending on the type of story being told. Standing or sitting can also be a means of communicating the story. Sitting allows you to lean forward, making eye contact easier, especially with children. Standing allows you to move around and even walk in toward your audience.

We all use nonverbal communication in our everyday lives. I remember from my childhood the look my mother gave me which I knew meant I'd better behave. Romance and love are often conveyed through body language. When my husband and I were dating, we could spend hours gazing into each other's eyes. The look of love you might say. Or that longing look as you say goodbye to a loved one as they board a plane. How about that angry look you receive after an argument? We tend to communicate a lot in nonverbal form.

For storytellers, facial expressions and hand gestures give the listener a visual to go along with the verbal telling and enhances the story's message. The quality of the storyteller's movements has a way of involving the audience in the story. If there are different characters in the story, body movement can help the audience distinguish between those characters. Expressive body movement is always a plus when telling to children. It keeps them engaged and helps in holding their attention.

Likewise, voice modulation is important in storytelling. The tone, attitude, pitch, rhythm, and emotion of your voice add to your story. The ebb and flow of your voice is important. The speed with which you speak in the story or the volume at which you tell is equally important. Warning: Sound effects are not wholeheartedly recommended. Not that you can't use them, but you must be careful, for sound effects can take your audience out of your story. They begin to anticipate the sound, not the words. Bringing them back into the story can be a challenge.

If you have a talent for voice characterization, use it. Being from the South, I will sometimes take a Southern story and dip into my Southern drawl to tell it. Depending on the story and the gender of the teller, a deep voice can be used if the character is a man or a high voice if the character is a woman. If the teller has a talent for different accents, these can add to the story and the enjoyment of the audience. Of course, there's nothing wrong with simply telling a story in your God-given voice.

Part 7

More About Storytelling

ALL GREAT STORIES DO THREE TERRIBLE THINGS.
- They disorient before they provide clarity or insight.
- They create anticipation before they defy expectations.
- They have one single clear thing the audience should take away.

Basic storytelling forms are like a rollercoaster. As a story progresses, the audience experiences the rise and the fall of the different parts of the story.

The protagonist, or main character, carries the audience through the story and is the most important. The antagonist, or villain, stands in the way of the hero.

For a story to feel satisfying to the audience, it's necessary for both the main character and his circumstances to change. This is called a story arc. For instance, if your protagonist begins as this clean-cut yet arrogant character, then perhaps at the end he's grubby and humble. Or if he begins as a drunk, he's gotta end up sober. A satisfying story is a story of change.

Remember conflict? Overall, people should not get along well in stories. Well, at least not during the entire story. Yet even with conflict there must be some sort of resolution. I'll be honest here—open-ended stories that offer no solution or closure drive me nuts. I'm one of those listeners and/or readers who want to see a story come to an end. For my ears and eyes when a story or book (usually books) leaves you hanging there must be a sequel in the mind of the teller or writer. Sequels are okay with me but only if the previous story had an end. It's okay to tease at the end, so that the audience lets out this collective sigh. That works. But don't leave everything unresolved.

Stories that we grew up with often had a common thread, especially at the beginning. Should you find yourself telling for a group of little kiddos, these phrases always captivate.

> Not so long ago in a country far away…
> Once upon a time there lived…
> Suddenly from out of nowhere came…
> I remember not so long ago…
> We could hardly believe our eyes…
> Eventually we…
> The next thing we knew we were…
> We could not believe what we'd heard…
> At last, we found…
> The moral of the story is…
> If only I'd known about…

The takeaway from this part of storytelling is:
1. Immersing your audience in the story.
2. Creating some sort of suspense.
3. Like writing, in oral storytelling, you must show not simply tell.
4. Engaging your audience by having them participate in the story. This is especially good when telling to children.
5. S.T.A.R. What's that? At the end of the story, the teller must give the audience <u>s</u>omething <u>t</u>hey'll <u>al</u>ways <u>r</u>emember.

Part 8

The Greatest Storyteller of All Time: Jesus

JESUS LOVED TO TELL STORIES. IN FACT, EXCEPT WITH HIS disciples, most of his teaching was through stories. In the Book of Matthew, the thirteenth chapter, we find seven parables, or stories that Jesus told to a crowd of people who gathered around Him. Jesus went out and sat by a lake. I'm assuming for some quiet time to think. But soon a large crowd gathered around Him. He got into a boat, sat down, and began to tell parables to the people on the shore.

His disciples couldn't understand why Jesus talked to the people in parables. His answer is in Matthew 13:11-17. "Because the knowledge of the secrets of the kingdom of heaven has been given to you, but not to them. Whoever has will be given more, and they will have an abundance. Whoever does not have, even what they have will be taken from them. This is why I speak to them in parables: 'Though seeing, they do not see; though hearing, they do not hear or understand.' In them is fulfilled the prophecy of Isaiah: 'You will be ever hearing but never understanding; you will be ever seeing but never perceiving. For this people's heart has become calloused; they hardly hear with their ears, and they have closed their eyes. Otherwise, they might see with their eyes, hear with their ears, understand with their hearts and turn, and I would heal them.' But blessed are your eyes because they see, and your ears because they hear. For truly I tell you, many prophets and righteous people longed to see what you see but did not see it, and to hear what you hear but did not hear it." Jesus then went on to explain the meaning of the first parable He'd told the people—The Parable of the Sower.

Whether telling the story of the farmer sowing seed, the Parable of the Weeds, the Mustard Seed, and the Yeast, or even the Parables of the Hidden Treasure and the Pearl, Jesus was an expert at communication. He utilized the vernacular of his time. The listener had to pay close attention not only to the words of Jesus but how He phrased and crafted each sentence and story.

It's interesting to see the concept of storytelling making a comeback in Christian circles. We see it in the rise of Christian fiction and films. We also see it highlighted in today's preaching style. The use of video clips to tell or show a short story has become quite commonplace in churches and ministries. Stories, well told and appropriately used, allow pastors and teachers to bring the truth of Scripture to life in a way that Roman numeral three, part B, number 2, simply can't convey.

There's a place for a story and a place for scholarship. Jesus was keenly aware of the difference between the two. His communication with the crowds through parables, highlighted in Matthew 13, provides such a great example for us.

Summary

ALL THE ELEMENTS OF PUTTING TOGETHER A GREAT STORY ARE found in the first half of this book. Whether you're looking at the art of oral storytelling just for fun or if you want to begin telling stories in a guild or event setting, these are the tools you'll want to carry with you.

Different Types of Storytelling

The Hook

The Myths and Truths of Storytelling

Structure of a Story and Parts of a Story

The Story Spine

Body Movement and Voice Inflection

Connecting with your audience

I hope you've learned some things you didn't already know. I hope when you're telling your stories you won't merely make the comment that the lady screamed. I hope you'll bring her on stage with you and let her scream. A little something I learned from some of Mark Twain's writings.

It's storytime!

The Many Faces of Storytelling

Welcome to my world of storytelling.

Following are personal stories written in my style. A little humor. A little satire.

Some I have told at various events.

They require my permission to retell or change to represent another teller's style.

Storytelling Ethics always apply when retelling stories that are published.

Some stories are in the public domain and are available to retell.

Should the story not be in the public domain, the teller should make every effort to obtain permission to tell the story.

If permission is granted, the teller should give credit to the author of the story and indicate that permission at the beginning of the story.

Enjoy!

Let's get into some stories..........

Story #1

A Girl Can Never Wear Too Much Blue Eye Shadow

The 1960s through the 1980s brought us the blue eye shadow craze. It's embarrassing to think I actually wore the stuff—and lots of it. In an effort to bring back this crazy craze, the fashion industry has renamed it. Now it's called sapphire or teal or aqua. From my point of view, it's still blue eye shadow.

I'm not sure what possessed girls from my era to deface their eyelids with this hideous war paint. There's no reason for it. In fact, it should have been illegal. We all looked ridiculous. But I guess we looked ridiculous together. Strength in numbers, as they say. So if you were going out in public wearing blue eye shadow, you better take a friend with you. And she had better be wearing it too.

It makes sense if a girl can never wear too much blue eye shadow, she can never have too many blue eyeshadow friends, either. All my friends stood firm in the belief if one of us was going to make a fashion statement, we all would make it. And there were many fashion statements to be made. From bandannas to mop-top hairstyles to bell-bottomed pants to mini-skirts to go-go boots to the widely popular bikini, my friends and I all participated in the trends of the sixties. I don't recall any of us getting on board with the pillbox hat thing, but we sure did like the psychedelic prints, highlighter colors, paisleys, and the many mismatched patterns. And who could forget polyester?

With the hippie movement in full swing, we all longed to be a part of it. However, those of us from my small corner of the world feared the wrath of our parents should we venture too close to that scene. The ever-popular Fourteenth Street in Atlanta, Georgia, beckoned my friends and me with its lure of free spirits wearing ponchos, moccasins, love beads, peace signs, headbands, and chain belts. We, however, made the wise decision to stick with the blue eye shadow and bell-bottomed pants. Freedom to cruise at will meant more to us than hanging with the hippies on Fourteenth Street.

Even though there were more than seventy-million teenagers in the United States in the 1960s due to the Baby Boom that occurred after World War II, my parents proved quite capable of keeping me in my place. Ditto with the parents of all my friends. The fact that there were so many of us never intimidated our parents one little bit. We only dared cruise the Varsity, a local landmark drive-in, to woo the boys with our flashy blue eye shadow and hippie-like ensembles.

My friends were my world during my teen years. We protected each other, stood by each other, cried with each other, and laughed ourselves into convulsions together. I'm sure if cell phones and computers had been around at that time we would have spent most of our lives grounded.

Of course the 1960s brought with it periods of violence and unrest as well. The Vietnam War was in full swing. Demonstrations at every turn. The assassinations of John F. Kennedy, Dr. Martin Luther King, Jr., and Bobby Kennedy filled the airways. As all this turmoil swirled around us, the necessity for friendship became all-important. My friends were my family. With them I could wear as much blue eye shadow as I wanted without the fear of ridicule.

At times we dressed up like hippies and crashed the local library. Or we strolled down the mall acting like fools with a political ax to grind, shooting peace signs at everyone like we knew what it meant. The overall feel of the times never occurred to us as we pranced around in our bell-bottomed pants, tie-died shirts, and heavily painted on blue eye shadow. We were simply friends standing as one. Blue eye shadow became our group symbol, our signature color, and our statement to the adults in our lives.

God not only watches over first-time parents, but He also watches over idiot teenagers who think themselves immortal. As I reflect on those times and realize we literally could have lost our lives, I cringe with fear. Not only at the thought of all of us becomimg statistics, but also because I have grandchildren who've reached that age or are fast approaching the age of stupidity. Riding through Georgia Tech University and attempting to pick up boys much older than ourselves could have ended in a tragedy none of us would have recovered from. We never considered that at the time. Obviously, our blue eye shadow had gone to our brains making us incapable of intelligent thought.

Now fifty years later, I finally know better. I'm not at all tempted to wear blue eye shadow, cruise the mall adorned in bell-bottomed pants, or even ride through the local university attempting to pick up boys older than I am. I've learned my lesson. And I owe it all to Bubba Dupriest.

I dated Bubba only once. Not because of his appearance or his character but because we almost died the night of our date. *Wait Until Dark* made its debut at the Fox Theatre in downtown Atlanta in January 1967. January in Atlanta is typically met with ice and snow. We all desperately wanted to see the movie and knew how cool it would be to brag we had gone *downtown*. Our parents had forbidden us to venture out in the ice and snow, warning us we could slide off a bridge and be killed. In particular, they warned us about traveling downtown. We didn't listen and lied to our parents as to where we were going that night.

By the time we arrived at the Fox Theatre, our nerves were spent. Our parents' warnings had almost become a reality. Not once but twice, our car came dangerously close to sliding off a bridge. The movie, although great, took a backseat to thoughts of trying to make it back home after the terrifying trip there.

I'm sure the four of us had visions of the police calling our parents with the news of our demise. As captivating as Audrey Hepburn and Efrem Zimbalist, Jr. were, we had a most difficult time paying attention. The reality of our disobedience came to a head when we left the theatre. We walked flatfooted to our car in an effort not to slip on the ice. Bubba looked back at me as he stepped off the curb onto the street and proceeded to fall flat on his back. I screamed and started crying so uncontrollably that my blue eye shadow started running down my face.

We all thought he had broken something important. Fortunately, the only thing broken was his pride. We eventually made it back home in one piece. Bubba never called to ask for another date. The fall had embarrassed him far too much. Even the blue eye shadow I had worn that night couldn't fix his bruised ego.

My friend tried to console my hurt feelings. Even though Bubba Dupriest could have never been the boy of my dreams, I secretly wanted to be the girl of his. Blue eye shadow notwithstanding.

Unlike all fads, true friends stay around. Even though time and miles have a way of wedging itself in between us, we stick together, even if only in spirit. We try to stay in touch by whatever means we have at our disposal because we know one day we won't be able to.

If the Story Fits Tell It

I can remember the pain in my mother's face when she would learn of yet another one of her friends' passing. The look of regret because she couldn't be there to say good-bye. Things like this tend to bring one's future into full focus.

I have found over the years that those I have chosen to call my friends are those I have chosen to love, appreciate, cherish, confide in, stand by, and fight for all the days of my life. As John 15:13 always reminds me, "Greater love hath no man than this, that a man lay down his life for his friends." Those friends are the keepers.

I'm sure the Apostle John did not know the importance of blue eye shadow at the time of his writings. For those of us who lived for the fads of the day and swore our allegiance to each other, blue eye shadow gave us the courage to make a statement far beyond the covering of our eyelids with this hideous color. Although I must admit I did truly love it at the time.

Life always seems to come full circle. God has a way of making us aware of the things in life that matter most. We come to the realization not only can we never have too many girlfriends, but a girl can never wear too much blue eye shadow.

Story #2

Basic Needs

Air-Water-Food
Shelter-Sleep

Remember in school when we learned about the five basic needs? You know the ones, right? Air, water, food, shelter, sleep. You certainly can't go too long without air. Three minutes tops. If you go beyond that, you're looking at brain damage. But what about water? Well, you can actually go about three days without water. Although not enough water equals dehydration, which leads to your blood getting thick. If that happens it becomes more difficult on the heart, which must work harder. And if the blood is too thick, it's difficult for it to flow.

As for food, you can live up to three weeks without food. Surprisingly you can only go about three hours without shelter. Why? The weather. Exposure to the elements can affect water loss in your body. Sleep—we all need sleep. A lack of sleep can be detrimental to your overall health. Loss of memory, headaches, hallucinations all can result from an extended lack of sleep.

So basic needs are important, yes? Then in walks COVID-19 taking away our basic needs. Or what we thought were our basic needs. It really didn't take away any of our *basic* needs because we still have air, water, food, shelter, sleep. Well, maybe sleep is in the deficit for some of us. Pre-COVID-19 we had just about everything we needed and wanted, right? We probably had more than we needed. Still, we wanted what we wanted, too. Almost everything fell under the essential category. In our minds anyway.

Now we're faced with the lack of toilet paper. It's essential, that's for sure. But now it's also become a luxury. How crazy is that? Tissues, paper towels, and paper napkins—also essentials. I found myself reaching into my stash of Christmas napkins to keep from using my regular paper napkins for fear I'd never find another paper napkin ever! These things were never important to me before. They were everyday items I could get at the store any time I needed or even wanted them.

Through all the days, weeks, and months of being unable to do the things we want and need to do, we've found that there are other basic needs we never thought were basic needs. We've also discovered there are many more nonessential things we thought were essential.

The biggest jolt to my system came in the form of my church closing its doors. I never in my wildest nightmare thought I'd ever see that happen. Then the closing of schools. My heart broke for the 2020 college and high school seniors who might never have the opportunity of walking across a stage and accepting their diploma. The little kindergarteners who began their learning journey only to have their graduation from kinder to "big" school halted. My own 50-year high school reunion? Canceled.

I also deeply felt the need to be around my grandchildren and children. To hug them and smooch their faces. The cancelation of our family Sunday dinners made me sad. Not being able to have our grandkids over just for fun or to have a sleepover. No special lunches or dinners out at our favorite restaurants. No movies. No library visits, for crying out loud. No playground fun. The need for exercise at our local gym, gone. And the need to shop? Okay, it's not a need but it's fun. And getting our hair cut.

How gut-wrenching is it to see people having to wave at their loved one through a window? Some of the elderly don't understand why this is happening. If a loved one becomes ill and must go to the hospital or must have an operation, you can't even be with them or visit them. The saddest, I think, is not being able to bury the dead. How does a person deal with not being able to have a funeral for their loved one who has passed?

Suddenly the basic needs thing has expanded. Let's face it, some things aren't basic needs. They are simply fun things. But those fun things are important to our emotional health. Can we live without the fun stuff or the extravagant stuff? Of course we can. Those are wants, not needs. But it doesn't make us miss them any less.

What then will we come away with after this is in our rearview mirror? Will we appreciate our loved ones more? Hug and kiss them more often? Will we appreciate the things we *do* have more and not long for the things we don't? When our church doors open will we be more thankful for our right to worship? Will we be more thankful for our rights in general?

For now, we sit at home, "sheltered in place" in some areas of the country and "stay at home" in other areas. What if we had no technology to help us reach out to one another? No video capabilities to see one another. No cell phones. No TV with nine million stations running 24/7. What if we just had to stay in our homes, alone or as a family? What would our basic needs be then? Well, they'd still be the same. Air, water, food, shelter, sleep. It might drive us mad, but we'd still be alive.

Pandemics can take your mind to the darkest of places. Dealing with the illness, the deaths, the possible financial collapse. The reality is we're fortunate to have technology. We can keep our spirits up through virtual viewing. Does it make up for the physical closeness? Absolutely not. Pandemics can also bring out the innovativeness of humans. Coping with the challenges. And sometimes it even brings people closer together in a realm of thankfulness.

I'm not sure how we will react when the world opens completely. We may go crazy. We may go forward awkwardly and shyly. I am sure, however, that we will come through it on a different level. We'll look at everything through a need to have lens. Our basic needs list may change. I know we'll never look at toilet paper the same.

A lot of my friends have said they appreciate things more. Some say they've enjoyed the quiet or the aloneness. Some say they've not been able to sleep. Some sleep too much or eat too much. Some say they've found they are more creative. I'm thinking we all just want our lives back to what they were before this evil fell over the world.

The Book of James tells us in James 1:12: "Blessed is the man who remains steadfast under trial, for when he has stood the test he will receive the crown of life, which God has promised to those who love him." And Romans 5:3-5 reads: "More than that, we rejoice in our sufferings, knowing that suffering produces endurance, and endurance produces character, and character produces hope, and hope does not put us to shame, because God's love has been poured into our hearts through the Holy Spirit who has been given to us."

Won't it be grand when we look back in a year, or even two, and remember how this time felt? Will our basic needs be the same as they were before? Will we be okay with just our basic needs?

Story #3

Dear Dishwasher

It appears you are never satisfied. When first we met, my life as an adult had just begun. You never seemed to mind how empty or full you were. I could leave you for days, never giving you a second thought. You never cared whether your dispenser contained tablets, gel packs, powder, or liquid. And you certainly never gave me any trouble when it came to your upper wash arm spinner, rack adjuster, or hinge cable. You were always so very low maintenance. I became enamored with your sleek looks. Sometimes I found myself just walking by you and stroking your handle in admiration. Looks and dependability—you were a dream come true. You even outshone some of my friends in that category.

I remember a time when people had to do their dishes—in a sink—using their own hands. How lucky am I to have such a companion? Why all I need do is push three simple buttons and magically my mess is completely cleaned up. Dare I even call you, dear dishwasher, a friend?

After I married and had children, I thought things between us would stay the same. I now know that to be a naïve assumption. You became more and more demanding, to the point of being ferocious. I found myself dreading our time together. I never knew from one moment to the next if you would even work. Do your job! Be there in my time of need! Isn't that the basis of any relationship? Being there in time of need? What happened to you? Why do you seem so self-absorbed?

It seems like yesterday when you were new, and it was just the two of us. You didn't mind if days went by and you sat idle. Now that I have a husband and kids you seem to want my constant attention. Filling you up and running you daily. I never seem to get any rest. I'm always having to deal with you.

And if that's not enough, now you've started to leak, costing me hundreds of dollars to get a repairman out just to look at you. Then more money to fix you. I thought that would be the end of it, but no. Suddenly you stopped working altogether.

I dumped more and more money into you. For what? Now that I have a family, isn't it your responsibility to keep up with the mounds of dirty dishes? Why must I always have to ask pretty please? When I had no kids or husband, you were there for me. Ready to clean my dishes. And with no complaints. Not so now.

You constantly complain by only cleaning half the dishes. How does that happen anyway? Don't get me started on the glasses. Spots everywhere. You never did that before. What has changed in your attitude? I can't help it if I fell in love, got married, and had kids. Why should that bother you? Is it because now you must work? Isn't that what you're supposed to do anyway? I didn't purchase you as an ornament, just to be looked at and admired. I purchased you to work!

Where do we go from here? Our relationship is definitely at the breaking point. I don't find you attractive any longer. In fact, I find you sloppy. There's no shine, no cleanliness, no excitement in you. I must admit to you now—I'm looking at other dishwashers. There! I said it. I'm looking to replace you. Don't bother asking what kind of dishwasher. And don't even think of asking what model. Let's just leave it at the fact that I'm looking.

I can't believe you're surprised. What good are you when I unload you then have to rewash the dishes? I mean, really! Take the other night, for instance. You, fully loaded, should have rejoiced in the knowledge that you had a family to serve. But, no. What did you do? You whined, then you sputtered, then you let out this gosh-awful sound followed by smoke that blew from your undercarriage! We had to call the fire department to extinguish you. To add insult to injury, the fire department cited *us* for not having a fire extinguisher in our house!

I'm so done with you. I'll not call you dear dishwasher any longer. It's over. Our relationship has ended. You brought this on yourself. You left me with no choice. I can no longer continue to put my hard-earned dollars into your upkeep. Your replacement will be here tomorrow.

My dear new dishwasher……

Story #4

Death Can Really Ruin Your Day

I've never been one to obsess over death. Sure, I've thought about it. But only in terms of cinematography. Take, for instance, the movie *Defending Your Life* with the main characters being Julia and Daniel. Both characters die, Daniel in a car wreck on his birthday and Julia in a pool, drowning after tripping. The way they both died didn't impress me. It was the review of *Julia's* life that did. She led a near-perfect life. Void of all selfishness. Full of generosity. Courage was her middle name. Now that's how I've always envisioned my death. Selfless, all the while being overly generous during a courageous act of heroism. Beautiful!

It's kind of like a motion picture of me rushing into a burning building never giving a care for my safety or my own life. Only one thought in mind: to save those trapped inside. Flames licking their way around every nook, cranny, and crevice. Me, fearless in my quest! Crying out the battle cry of heroes as I fight tirelessly to the death!

When you look at the word death, on the surface you must admit, it's pretty scary. For a five-letter word, it does carry a punch. If you look it up in the dictionary, you'll find the definition is scary as well. It seems quite final.

Now let's take that same word—death—still kinda scary, right? However, for a believer in Christ, people like me, death is like a peaceful sleep. Not as scary. The Bible speaks to death and presents it to the reader in two types. Physical death and spiritual death. Let's face it, we're all going to experience physical death. It's unavoidable. But spiritual death is an altogether different subject. The Bible is absolute in its explanation regarding spiritual death. Because after our physical death, it's time to face God and His judgment.

When loved ones die, if we know our loved one to be a Christian, the mourning we go through is certainly not for them, because remember it's just physical death. The mourning is for ourselves, because we know or fear what our lives will be like without them. We mourn the loss of their presence, and that pain we feel is the knowledge that we won't have them with us in this life.

I haven't always known that. My Aunt Virginia taught me that during the loss of her only child. But I didn't learn it immediately. It took years of watching her deal with that loss. And still, I didn't learn it until after she died. Until I sat at her funeral and reflected on her courage during the months and years that passed after her son's murder. Let me make this very plain. I do *not* possess that kind of courage, and God is fully aware of that fact. However, I also know that God will never allow me to stand alone. So death, although a serious matter, is not the end for those of us who believe in the one true God.

Which brings me back to my death plans. God is laughing now. Laughter is always good when situations become too heavy or too serious. It brings into perspective that which we rail against. Facing one's death, however, can be a bit daunting. Lights out! Curtain down! It never occurred to me that life might end while sitting on the toilet. Whoever said God doesn't have a sense of humor was wrong. He does!

One might think I would have learned that compelling lesson by now. I'm a whole lotta years into this thing I lovingly call life. It's not enough that I have a cinematographic vision of a heroic death all planned out in my mind, but I have verbalized it to friends and family members. After the snickers and laughter died down, they saw it my way.

If the Story Fits Tell It

Imagine my surprise when one night, one ordinary night, my life almost ended. And there wasn't even that infamous quintessential light that draws you in, where loved ones line each side of a magnificent corridor welcoming you as you walk toward that other world. No, no. My life almost ended with me lodged in between the toilet bowl and the wall of my master bathroom's water closet.

Luckily for me, my knight in shining armor slept peacefully in the next room and upon awakening to what must have sounded like the shower stall falling through the floor, came rushing in on his white horse to my rescue. Imagine the look on his face when he saw me on the floor in a somewhat contorted position. Belly down with my face flush up against the back wall. Looking as though my neck might be broken. So unladylike.

The only thing I remembered was having to pee at two o'clock in the morning. Getting up, walking to the toilet, and sitting down. The next thing I knew I was on the floor and my knight in shining armor was holding me in his arms attempting to get me to focus. Bless his heart!

I had stopped breathing. Right there next to the toilet bowl. Go ahead and laugh. It's okay. I know. Had my knight in shining armor not been scared out of his mind, he might have given up a chuckle or two. I'm quite certain that like the visions of sugar plums that danced in the heads of the sleeping children on Christmas Eve, he was having visions of dirty laundry dancing in his head and the prospect of having to wash his own undies. That can be a scary thought for a guy.

After several puffs in the mouth, the breath of life went rushing through my lungs as I gasped for that precious lifeline called oxygen. With one fell swoop, my knight in shining armor picked me up in his powerful arms and whisked me to our bed. Ooops, *Harlequin Romance* alert! Just kidding!

Seconds later, six larger than life angels surrounded my bed, checking my vitals, asking me questions, pricking my finger, and talking in whispers to my knight in shining armor. I later learned my answers to their questions were a bit off the mark, and not wanting to alarm me in my already confused state, the angels thought it appropriate to whisper their concerns.

Outside, the great chariot waited patiently with red lights softly blinking and spinning around in the cold dark night. I didn't even have an audience as the six larger than life angels lifted me ever so gently into the chariot. Once inside, I felt the warmth of the chariot's belly as I drifted in and out of sleep, only to awaken violently by a wave of nausea that sent my feet hurling through my mouth! It was a sad state of affairs. I could feel death hovering over the chariot, and I wasn't even dressed properly to greet it. My cinematographic vision of a heroic death was being met with me in my pajamas now decorated with the remnants of that night's dinner.

As the great chariot pulled up to the heavenly mansion, I was greeted by more beautiful angels who began sticking me with needles, squeezing my arm, pulling off my beautifully decorated pajamas and replacing them with cold, paper-thin robes that seemed to have the same sort of design on them. If that wasn't enough, they began to put sticky things all over my body and fastened wires into them. Before I knew it, they whisked me away to a room that looked more like the Holland Tunnel than an exam room. It housed a gigantic machine that the angels promptly stuck my head inside. They told me not to breathe, which seemed odd since only moments ago my knight in shining armor was screaming, "Breathe! Breathe!" But by this time, I was too tired to argue. I had to get ready. Death was hovering overhead, circling the heavenly mansion like a kettle of vultures waiting to feast on my flesh.

Funny, in the past, I hadn't pictured death as being vultures. I had always envisioned death as looking a lot more handsome than my visions that night. For some reason, my thoughts turned toward the evil-looking shadows that snatch up the bad people and take them off to places not spoken about in polite company. It must have been the nausea.

Certainly, death would look more like the handsome guy in the movies who portrayed it; all dressed in a million-dollar suit, buttoned-down crisp white starched shirt, and red tie signifying power. Standing by your bed looking down at you as if it were a long-lost friend come to pay their last respects.

Hours passed. As I waited for death to appear, nausea returned once again with a vengeance. The beautiful angels returned with potions that drove the nausea away and along with it, death. My knight in shining armor never left my side. I awoke in the heavenly mansion to the same loving face I saw while lying prostrate on my cold bathroom floor.

When the beautiful angels returned, I no longer had the hue of wallpaper paste. Life's rosy promising future had replaced death's gray dreary tone. And what a good thing, too. Imagine my relief to know that my gravestone would *not* read, "Beloved wife, mother, and grandmother. Died while sitting on the toilet."

Story #5

Does Anyone Really Know Polk Salad Annie?

BEING A PRODUCT OF THE SIXTIES, I KNEW THE SONG ENTITLED "Polk Salad Annie" well. It was written by a guy named Tony Joe White, an American singer-songwriter and guitarist best known for this song with the strange title. Sadly, Tony Joe passed away in 2018. He wrote other songs with alluring titles like "Rainy Night in Georgia" and "Steamy Windows." Tony Joe grew up on a cotton farm near a town called Oak Grove, in Louisiana. Cotton farming held a strong place in my family. It's back-breaking work. Not kind on the hands either. My uncle had a cotton farm that holds many memories for me. But then, that's a story for another time.

As a teenager, I found myself drawn to "Polk Salad Annie." I particularly liked one lyric which goes like this, "Polk Salad Annie 'Gators got you granny. Chomp, chomp, chomp." Don't get me wrong. I didn't suffer from some sick thought of a gator eating my granny. I simply loved the way the lyric flowed out of Tony Joe's mouth and the attitude with which he sang it. He had a way about him, his Louisiana drawl making the words all run together but somehow intelligible. His voice had this smoky texture with a touch of the blues that made the listener settle down into their soul. I thought Tony Joe White might be the coolest guy I'd ever seen—maybe even cooler than Elvis.

Now Tony Joe White not only *sang* "Polk Salad Annie," he *told* the story of this girl left to fend for herself during a time when people could scarcely find enough food. She had a no-account daddy, worthless brothers, and a mother who worked on the chain-gang. Not only that, according to the song, everybody knew Polk Salad Annie's mother to be "a wretched, spiteful, straight-razor-totin' woman."

Due to her circumstances, Polk Salad Annie had to do all

the cooking, which meant many meals of polk salad. Anybody with a lick of common Southern sense knows polk salad is toxic if not cooked properly. I mean, you've got to rinse this stuff at least twice to get rid of the harmful poison. Then you've got to boil it, and then rinse it again. After that, you've got to cook it in bacon fat or lard with onions or eggs. So you can't be fooling around when you decide you want a mess of polk salad. If you do, you just might find yourself knocking on the front door of the Pearly Gates before you were planning on it.

I'm confident I knew Polk Salad Annie at one time in my life. You see, I spent every summer of my growing up years in North Carolina, visiting my grandparents. Those visits were the times my parents cherished because it meant time away from an overactive kid who tended to drive them up the wall most every day. I truly hated it when the time came to go home. Being an only child in a sea of adults most always sucked.

Looking back over the summers I spent in North Carolina, I remember my cousins and I whispering about the people who lived in the house down the dirt road from my grandfather's farm. A shack might describe it better. Two parents and nine kids lived in that dilapidated old place consisting of only two bedrooms, a rundown kitchen, and a makeshift living room. No indoor bathroom—only an outhouse. My grandfather owned the only house in that area with indoor facilities.

I'm convinced the mother of those nine kids had to be the mother talked about in the song. Her only missing attribute being she didn't work on the chain-gang. My cousins and I were terrified of this mean, wretched, spiteful, woman who we all thought to be packing a straight-razor under her skirt. "No account" all but described the daddy.

I remember two of the nine kids quite vividly. The first

being a boy who made eyes at me every time he came for a visit to my grandfather's house. The second being his older sister who dressed in overalls that were always dirty. She had long, ratty blonde hair. I don't think she ever washed it. My grandmother didn't allow her to visit. She thought her too wild to be around me since I already leaned in that direction anyway.

The fact that my grandmother wouldn't allow this wild child in her house didn't deter me one little bit from sneaking out to play with her. Truth be known, I didn't much mind her brother making eyes at me. So on our adventures together we let him tag along. My youngest cousin threatened to tell our grandmother, which allowed her to weasel her way into our pack.

We tried desperately to stay out of trouble, but it never worked out that way. The wretched, spiteful, straight-razor-totin' woman always seemed to catch us. I can still see her in my mind, chasing us through the fields wielding the belt I'm sure she must have stolen from some unsuspecting merchant in town. We could feel the buckle whizzing past us, missing our heads by a fraction of an inch.

It didn't take long for me to realize I had stepped into a world unfamiliar to me. My summertime friends, although quite exciting, weren't like the friends I hung around with at school. These people lived on the edge of poverty—a word whose meaning I had no way of grasping at the time. Try as I might, I couldn't understand why I found myself drawn to people with whom I shared no common ground—either in my home life or my upbringing.

Our relationship ended abruptly when my older cousin told my grandparents about my secret friendship with the wild and dirty girl who lived in the rundown old shack. My older cousin was always a dirty rotten tattletale anyway. I'm still not sure I've ever forgiven him for it.

When "Polk Salad Annie" hit the charts and I heard the lyrics, I thought back to the summers I'd spent with my grandparents. The dirt road in front of their house that led to the dilapidated, old shack we all feared. Memories of the dirty little girl my grandmother never allowed in her house. The actual fondness I felt for the little boy who made eyes at me and covered my head so his mother's belt buckle wouldn't hit me those times she chased us through the fields. As I listened to the words sung by the great Tony Joe White, it occurred to me that I had really known Polk Salad Annie. And she lived right down the road from my grandparents.

Story #6

Don't Try to Perm Your Own Hair & Never Wear High-Heels on a Soggy Lawn

The time I tried to perm my hair turned into a disaster. I'd seen it done on T.V., so I figured I could do the same. My mother warned me that perming my own hair might not turn out as I envisioned it. Of course, I didn't listen to her because I knew better. They wouldn't just tell you on T.V. you could do something and it not be true, right? So I did it.

If ever there was a time when I wanted to shave every hair off my head that was the time. I looked like more than a deranged poodle; I looked like I'd stuck my entire head in an electrical socket. I cried for weeks. Not only because I looked ridiculous, but because my mother made me go to school and church anyway. Don't they put parents in jail for that?

As for high-heels, well, let's just say I don't wear them. My mother did. She had a million shoes, I'm sure of it. High-heels took center stage in her world. Since she was a shoe expert, particularly in regards to high-heels, she always warned against wearing them on a soggy lawn. They stick, she warned, far into the ground. A person could seriously injure themselves attempting to walk across a soggy lawn in high-heels. Wonder how she knew this. My theory is she tried it only to find herself face down on a soggy lawn. What I wouldn't have given to see that!

Our parents, mothers, in particular, offer up their advice to steer us in the right direction. Not really. They try to scare the yogurt out of us. My mother had to be the queen of telling me the scariest, vilest things ever conceived to persuade me not to do the things she didn't want me to do.

I have concluded one of the reasons we mothers repeatedly warn our kids about all the pitfalls of life, like perming your own hair, is because it's our way of telling them how very much we love them. My mother did all the yelling. My daddy never had to because he held the ultimate power.

Does one ever enjoy doing what our parents tell us? I know I resented it tremendously. My mother knew this. My daddy had little concern for whether or not I resented his discipline. Why would he? He was a drill sergeant in the Army. Mother *did* care, and made sure I understood the reasons behind her warnings. And, as I've written about and spoken about before, she put the mother's curse on me. Meaning: *I hope your children act just like you!* Don't doubt it doesn't work, because it does. My kids were every bit the image of me. Hence the never-ending smirk on my mother's face when I'd tell her of their antics.

There are some things our mothers tell us that ring true. Things like: *You only have one chance to make a first impression. You will understand when you have children.* And, *High School won't kill you.* I heard that last one a lot as I actually *did* think High School would kill me.

If I'm honest about my past and the things I did, like perming my own hair, I'd share all the things my mother warned me about and how those things turned out when I didn't listen to her warnings. Oh, wait! I did do that. Chapter twelve in my book *Anyone Seen My Rose-colored Glasses?* that's titled "The Reason Doing It My Way Doesn't Work." Yes, there were many examples there. Twelve to be exact.

Years later, we laughed when we reminisced about the times she warned me of pending disasters. The times I listened, and the times I didn't. The times I did it my way while my parents sat back and watched as I failed miserably. Ironically, they were always there to pick up the pieces. But then they would send me forward to clean up the rest.

There's great wisdom in not trying to perm your own hair. The fear alone of ending up looking like a cartoon character is good enough for me. There's even greater wisdom in never wearing high-heels on a soggy lawn. Once those heels get stuck—you ain't goin' anywhere.

That's the main point, I think. Our mothers' warnings were made to move us forward, toward independence, and not keep us bogged down in the mire of life. And even though I never cracked my head open or even got warts from playing with toads, I did learn responsibility and loyalty. I also learned hard work pays off.

The church played a huge part in my life growing up. My mother made sure of that. Daddy became disheartened in the church and left it up to my mother to take me. Not to worry, though. Daddy eventually changed his position. But through my mother's warnings—and ignoring those warnings—I learned that actions have consequences. I learned that God is always there for us. I learned He also allows us to fail. I learned the act of leaning on God and allowing Him to walk alongside me.

For those who allow God to walk with them through their decision making, theirs is a much easier path. For those of us who tend, on occasion, to ignore God's offer of assistance and our mother's warnings? Well, our paths tend to get rockier. In our defense, those rockier times make us realize the reason that doing it our way doesn't work. Just like trying to perm your own hair or wearing high heels on a soggy lawn, the outcome is usually disastrous.

Story #7

Dreamin' BIG and Livin' LARGE

The Way to Victory?

There's nothing wrong with dreaming big and living large. It's the American Dream, right? Is the American Dream alive even in unprecedented times? Those who dream big and find success in their dreams deserve to live large, don't you agree? In a country that is free and runs on capitalism, not socialism, Marxism, or communism, dreaming big and living large is your right, yes? Human beings have died for that right. That right, or freedom, affords you both luxuries.

In a time when little by little our freedoms are being taken away from us, dreaming big and living large is no longer a goal worth striving toward. I am not a defeatist, trust me. I do know, however, that the "one voice" thing can, at times, be highly overrated. I shudder to think of the United States of America that's run by people who think they know what's best for me and think nothing of taking away my rights to make decisions on my behalf. Then it's cloaked under the veil of unprecedented times. The words of Thomas Jefferson haunt me daily. He said, "Government big enough to supply everything you need is big enough to take everything you have. The course of history shows that as a government grows, liberty decreases." Well, that's a sobering and scary thought.

So how exactly does this work? You have a dream. It may be a little dream or a big dream. You put it down on paper just to see how it looks written out. Then you tape it to the mirror because you know you're going to be looking there every day. Now you step back and take a good long look at your dream. Looks pretty good. Each day when you look at your dream, you read it aloud just to hear the words spoken. It sounds pretty good.

Now that you've taken the time to dream, it's time to work. Work. That can be a scary word to some. Particularly those who believe in entitlements or unprecedented times. Let's look at the meaning of the word *work* just for grins. We know to work one must exert oneself. Put forth an effort. We must labor or toil. We must take on a task. Well now, there it is. All things foreign in a world of entitlements and bailouts.

Work takes time. That's another concept that some find difficult to grasp. My daddy always told me that anything worth having is worth working for. Imagine that. So for a dream to come to fruition, one must work toward that dream. Let's look at the definition of the word *dream*. That word conjures up images or thoughts played out in your head. We can dream awake or asleep, because when we dream these visions come up involuntarily. Dreams also bring forth goals or aspirations. Sounds all so dreamy does it not? Dreams are good. They give us something to reach for along the way.

When I was a little girl, I had grand expectations. Dreams, if you will, of becoming all sorts of magnificent things. Those dreams changed as I realized the work involved with accomplishing them. Dreams that dropped by the wayside because I thought I was either too limited in my abilities or not mentally equipped to accomplish the work.

Know what I say to that now? Hogwash! I had all the capabilities and opportunities available to me, as does anyone walking or breathing. The truth is, I was either too lazy, not interested enough in the dream, or I didn't want it bad enough to put forth the effort to accomplish it. Some would argue that an individual's circumstances have everything to do with whether they can accomplish their dream. Know what I say to that? Hogwash! Circumstances have nothing to do with anything.

One's true dream is worth the work, pain, and sacrifice required to accomplish it. Even during the unprecedented times we keep hearing about.

"Those people who will not be governed by God will be ruled by tyrants," said William Penn. Wise man. I'm truly not interested in being ruled by tyrants. I've seen that kind of ruling and it doesn't sit well with me.

What about that ever-popular term "unprecedented times." Like the time FDR got elected for a fourth term—unprecedented. Or reports that humans are transforming the landscape of the earth so fast—unprecedented. Or when the Senate passes the largest aid package in history—unprecedented. How about the stock market crash of 1929 when the Dow Jones Industrial Average dropped so much they called it the worst decline in U.S. history? Unprecedented. Then there's the Great Storm of 1900, considered the deadliest natural disaster in United States history, that occurred in Galveston, TX—unprecedented. Currently, as I'm writing this story, we're dealing with COVID-19—unprecedented we're told.

Unprecedented events in the Bible:

(Numbers 16:30-31) But if God does something unprecedented—if the ground opens up and swallows the lot of them and they are pitched alive into Sheol—then you'll know that these men have been insolent with God."

(Isaiah 13:8) Terror will seize them, pain and anguish will grip them; they will writhe like a woman in labor. They will look aghast at each other, their faces aflame. (from the effects of the unprecedented warfare)

(Act 17:19) Then they took him and brought him to a

meeting of the Areopagus, where they said to him, "May we know what this new teaching is that you are presenting? (unheard of and unprecedented)

So, when you're on your way to victory in your effort to dream big and live large, unprecedented things get in the way. Makes it tough, yes? Certainly. But it doesn't make it impossible. Unprecedented only means you've never done a certain thing before. Or you've never known about it before.

Walt Disney had his share of failures. He experienced a sad childhood and several business failures and setbacks. Henry Ford had several failures including bankruptcy along with a failed attempt at a political career. I'm sure they both experienced unprecedented times that led to not only their failures but probably to their many successes as well.

I submit that in unprecedented times, when our dreams seem out of reach, that we remember all the unprecedented times in history. As we look back at those times or we look at the time we're living through, we continue to move forward with the understanding that **Dreamin' BIG and Livin' LARGE** is okay. The road to victory is still possible. You may have to go into that unchartered territory, but that's the fun of it. Unprecedented times will either make you or break you.

Story #8

Elizabeth Marie Hutchinson

The Character Behind the Character

WHAT A CHARACTER THIS CHARACTER IS. ELIZABETH MARIE Hutchinson is the protagonist of my *When I Dream* series of children's books. When I started thinking about what kind of character Elizabeth needed to be, I thought, at the very least she should have freckles and naturally curly red hair. Well, maybe a little more substance than that. But the red hair—a must.

You're asking yourself why red hair, right? Because red hair is beautiful. That's it you ask? No, that's not it. The fact is that for a kid to have red hair both parents must carry the mutated MC1R gene. Now if they don't have red hair or one of them doesn't have red hair, the chances of them having a redheaded kid is about 25%. Plus, if you didn't know, less than 2% of the world's (that's right *the world's*) population have red hair. Crazy, yes? If you have red hair, not a good idea to try and color it. The pigment in red hair is tighter than any of the other hair colors, so you gotta strip it to color it. YIKES! Red hair is also thicker than other colors. I'm jealous!

Now for the bad news. Redheads *are* more susceptible to skin cancer, mainly because they have fairer skin. But then there's good news—redheads don't go grey. I'm lovin' that! And, they can produce their own Vitamin D. Lovin' that too! A bit of trivia is that redheads are more likely to be left-handed. On those facts alone I knew Elizabeth had to be a redhead.

In spite of the facts, there are silly myths about redheads. One is that they are witches, and when they die, they turn into vampires. I think not. Another myth is that they are unlucky.

I'm not buying that one at all. They have red hot tempers. Well, that one might not be a myth, considering the redheads in my family. Another silly myth is that bees sting them more than others, and they bruise more easily. Not true.

Since I'm the creator of this fictional character I got to choose the physical appearance. And Elizabeth being a redhead was not up for debate. But the funny thing about Elizabeth is that I created her well over thirty-five years ago. At that time, I didn't know I would one day have a purely redheaded granddaughter. I did know, however, that my grandfather on my daddy's side had strawberry blonde hair. I also knew that when my daddy grew a beard it did not match the color of his hair. The beard—red! The hair—black!

I also knew from the start that Elizabeth should be an only child. Authors, especially in the beginning stages of their writing career, typically write about what they know. And I knew all too well what it's like to be an only child.

Being an only child is in a category all its own. When people learn I'm an only child, I've had them tell me, "I never would have guessed. You don't act like an only child." Now I used to wonder what, exactly, that meant. Was it a good thing or a bad thing? I soon discovered they meant it in a good way. Kind of a round-about way of saying, "You're not a brat!" So, I knew Elizabeth's character needed to incorporate that non-bratty characteristic.

Elizabeth Marie Hutchinson is a young girl with a very vivid imagination. I think that comes with being an only child. Given that Elizabeth has no brothers and sisters to bug her or get into her stuff, she finds that she daydreams—a lot! Sometimes it gets her into trouble because she's daydreaming when she should be paying attention.

The part I love the most about Elizabeth is that she cherishes her friends. That, too, comes with being an only child. Even at a young age, Elizabeth knows the meaning of friendship. She understands what it means to call someone your friend. This makes Elizabeth's character extremely special.

She loves her friends more than she loves herself. Their happiness is her happiness. Their troubles are her troubles. She's always there when her friends are in need. She tries to see the good in others even when there seems to be no good at all. Take for instance, Margaret Callahan. Now there's a test of one's resolve. Elizabeth's challenge to find the good in Margaret came at a time when Margaret's self-absorbed ego had hit a high point. Only Elizabeth had the character it took to break down the barriers that kept Margaret from being the person she needed to be.

The other part of Elizabeth that I love is her love and respect for her family. Her mom and dad mean the world to her. She cares what they think. Especially what they think of her. It doesn't mean she never gets in trouble. It just means that when she does, it bothers her. The last thing she ever wants to do is to disappoint her parents. The best part is that Elizabeth shares her thoughts and her life outside of the Hutchinson home with her parents. She asks for their advice and guidance. And they give it freely—especially Mr. Hutchinson.

But the other good part about Elizabeth is that she listens. She understands that although parents can be a real pain, they are usually right about most things. Elizabeth also knows that her parents love her and strive to do those things that are in Elizabeth's best interest. And although she sometimes doesn't agree with them, she honors their authority as her parents. That's an amazing characteristic for a kid.

Elizabeth also has a very curious side to her character. You might even say she's a bit nosey. Sometimes her need to fix things causes her friends to wonder where one of Elizabeth's schemes might lead. But her heart is always in the right place. Even when she tries her hand at being a detective!

Elizabeth's imagination and her dreams come together magically. The magic takes her to a place where she finds counsel when things in her life seem impossible to figure out. Although she knows the importance of her parents in her life, there are some things she needs extraordinary help with. Magical if you will.

As I started developing the character of Elizabeth, I wanted her to appeal to all the children who read about her. I wanted them to feel as though Elizabeth could easily be their friend. I needed to come up with one word that would sum up Elizabeth's character. I decided that word would be: Charming. That *magic* effect that makes people like her. Elizabeth is the best person to have on your side. She's a loyal friend. And don't we all need a loyal friend sometime in our life?

STORY #9

HAPPY BIRTHDAY SWEET SIXTEEN

I'M NOT SURE HOW IT HAPPENED THAT MY OLDEST CHILD IS knocking on the door of fifty. Surely yesterday I brought her home from the hospital. The next day she cut her first tooth. After that, she crawled, then walked. Then we celebrated birthday number one. And before we knew it, we were singing, "Happy Birthday Sweet Sixteen."

So where did all those years in between go? I must have been in a coma these many years since we watched as she backed down the driveway and onto the street, driving solo on that day she turned sixteen.

I can still remember her not being an easy pregnancy. The triple sickness days—morning, noon, and night—almost did me in. This child made sure I remembered every day we spent together because the sickness didn't last a couple of months. It lasted nine long months.

Come to think of it, the delivery wasn't very pleasant either. After decking two nurses and kicking my doctor in the face, they strapped me down. They called the drug *twilight*. Like one of those vampire novels or something. Only they weren't around then. I guess you could say I resembled a vampire by the time the drug kicked in. When that part ended, they brought me the most precious bundle of joy I'd ever seen. All decked out with olive skin, the blackest of hair, and eyes as dark as coal. Plus, she had all her fingers and toes. I counted.

I'm not sure when I got it into my head to become a mother. How does any nineteen-year-old decide they're mature enough to take on the responsibility of parenthood? Only the incredibly dumb ones I suspect. The father decided early on, even though we were married, he certainly didn't want that kind of responsibility. And so, my daughter and I gutted it out together. Learning as we went along. On-the-job training is what it's called. We grew up together, experiencing all the bumps and bruises that go along with childhood.

We faced the terrible twos when nothing on my coffee table remained safe. The tantrums that resulted from not getting one's way. I'm not referring to her, I'm referring to me. Somehow, we survived that.

As time went by, we dealt with losing her first tooth and being afraid kids would call her snaggle tooth.

The trauma of her first love. The little boy known as *the one*. You know that guy. The one who makes your heart go pitter-pat. The one who winks at you and causes your heart to melt. The one who blows you a kiss across the classroom. The one who carries your books. The one who dumps you for your best friend. You know that guy, right?

All the drama that comes with middle school. The hormones surging through her body. Days of joy that suddenly turn to days of tears, happens within moments of one another. Uncomfortable questions about sex. Dealing with the first period.

As difficult as it tended to get from time to time, I'm not so sure I'd go back and change a thing. I know now that God watched over us throughout those years. He made sure we made it through every challenge and never wavering with His unconditional love for us both.

Throughout the years I discovered that trials and tribulations are the side effects of being a parent. Now I sit back and marvel at the woman she has become. Wife, mother, business owner, and all-around magnificent human being. I'd like to think I had a small part in that last one. I like her very much.

If the Story Fits Tell It

It's never fun letting go. But we must when it pertains to our children. I've come to believe the reason it's so difficult is that at that point we no longer have any power. We must fall back on what we've taught them and pray we told them the right things. I also think it makes us consider our own mortality. It forces us to take stock in our own lives. How stinkin' scary is that?

Happy Birthday, Sweet Sixteen. It's a time I'll never forget. A time I'll forever cherish. A time when one candle on the birthday cake suddenly became sixteen.

Regardless of all the candles since, she'll always be my baby girl.

Story #10

If It's Not One Thing It's Your Mother

MOTHERS AND DAUGHTERS ARE ONE OF THE MOST COMPLICATED relationships known to womankind. It's not like you can just smack your mother in the face and walk away like you can a guy. Where does one begin to explain how to get along with one's mother?

I know my relationship with my mother was tumultuous at best—particularly during my adolescent years. Freeze frame of a time with my mother: (all caps to indicate yelling)

"DON'T YOU DARE DO THAT!"

"ALL MY FRIENDS DO IT!"

"I DON'T CARE WHAT ALL YOUR FRIENDS DO! YOU ARE MY CHILD!"

"I HATE YOU! YOU NEVER LET ME DO ANYTHING!"

"DON'T TALK TO ME THAT WAY! GO TO YOUR ROOM!"

I spent a lot of hours in my room.

Being an only child meant I spent more hours than I care to even remember in the presence of adults. I hated every stinkin' second of it. From the time I was a little girl until I became a teenager, I cringed at the thought of another *Stone Family* outing. What were these two people thinking? You know, the ones who called themselves my parents? The same people who took a vow to care for me, educate me, feed me, house me, and clothe me. Who were they anyway? I never asked to be born!

For years I plotted ways to escape from this prison consisting of nothing but old people. The ones who pinch your cheeks and utter stupid remarks like, "You've just grown so much. Not mommy and daddy's little girl anymore! You're just the sweetest little thing! And oh, look you've gotten your boobies!" Ugh! To add insult to injury, my parents stood idly by smiling like two drunken fools allowing this child abuse to occur. My mother being the biggest offender.

After a while, my dad just dropped out of the picture, especially during my adolescent years. Had I been a boy, he most likely would have stayed in place with my mother being the one to drop out. Given my gender, it became necessary for my mother to take over as primary parental disciplinarian. Oh, don't think for a second that she didn't threaten me repeatedly with the presence of my father and his wrath. Little did she know he wanted no part of dealing with me. Still, she believed it necessary to instill in me her thoughts regarding womanhood and all that went with being a true Southern lady. From that point on my life changed.

It all started when I turned five and my mother discovered her only daughter—her only child—hated girly girl things. Much to my dismay, I became known as the kid whose mother was hell-bent on turning her into a girly girl.

The first thing my mother did to me to turn me into her *precious little Southern belle* came in the form of how she dressed me. Lace and frills and bows and all. She decided to sign me up to appear on the *Howdy Doody Show*, never imagining how that might turn out. I write about this experience in my book *Anyone Seen My Rose-colored Glasses?* I guess you'll have to get a copy to find out how that went down.

As I grew into my adolescent years, my father began sleeping and eating at the NCO club. Not because my mother threw him out of the house, but because my mother chose mealtimes to share with me her thoughts on sex, drugs, and rock 'n roll. My father could handle the drugs and some of the rock 'n roll talk. It was the sex part that made him break out in hives. All my mother's warnings suddenly fell under the heading of *all the stupid things your mother used to tell you!*

As time passed, I eventually grew up and got married. Soon after, God's sense of humor kicked in and He blessed me with three daughters. Throughout their growing up years, I found myself talking and acting like my mother. In turn, my three daughters talked and acted like me.

Now my daughters have all grown. My mother lived with me for a little over eight years. During that time, we had our battles. She listened to crazy music, stayed up to all hours of the night with her television blasting, ate all sorts of junk food, and wouldn't eat her broccoli. The tables indeed turned. She had become that which she previously scorned me for being. I found myself scorning her for acting like I did when I was her child.

I know now, as I did then, that my mother always loved me. She always wanted what she thought best for me. Even when I had her as a substitute teacher in third grade and she gave me a **_D_** in conduct! And the time she made me wear a dress to Marcie Jernigan's birthday party when she knew I hated dresses! And the time she made me kiss old Aunt Mildred on the check when she knew I hated old Aunt Mildred! And the time she made me eat Brussels sprouts because she said they were good for me when she knew I hated Brussels sprouts! Mothers and daughters. How do we survive each other's personalities?

Now that my mother is gone, I find myself looking back. All the time I wasted not listening to her. All the times she didn't listen to me. Granted I paid less attention to her than she to me. The same applies to my daughters. We all go through that time when all we want to do is block out the voice that insists on telling us what to do. But I also realize that as mothers and daughters we usually grow toward a different relationship. One that brings us to the point where we start to like one another.

Funny how I catch myself saying some of the same things Mother used to say. Funnier how when she said them, I didn't think much of them. The wisdom of her thoughts escaped me. I don't think that now.

"TURN DOWN THAT GOSH AWFUL MUSIC!"

"IT'S NOT THAT LOUD, MOTHER!"

"YOU'RE GOING TO GO DEAF IF YOU KEEP PLAYING IT THAT LOUD?"

"WHAT?"

"I SAID, YOU'RE GOING TO GO DEAF! ARE YOU BEING A SMART ALECK?"

"NO, MOTHER!"

"SEE THAT YOU AREN'T!"

"YES, MOTHER."

I almost miss those times. Those crazy adolescent times. Those times when there seemed to be more friction between us than harmony. More clashing of the Titans than peace among the natives. But why would there be? Mothers and daughters are that rash just below the skin that when scratched flares up and gets ugly. Ultimately, we find our way.

Admittedly I've asked God why the dance? Why must we always step on rocks before finding a smooth road? God laughs and says, "To make life interesting."

My mother's face appears. She's smiling. Is it any wonder? If it's not one thing it's your mother!

Story #11

Imperfections

THE IMPERFECTIONS THAT MAKE US PERFECT FOR ONE ANOTHER are many. Just look at Beauty and the Beast. The guy was a beast, for crying out loud. The girl a beauty. How in all that's sane could a beauty fall in love with a beast? His breath alone could stop an elephant in its tracks. Talk about imperfections. But love him she did.

My husband snores like a freight train. It drives me mad. It interrupts my sleep. It makes me angry. I have visions of smothering him with my pillow. And I won't even get into the other bodily functions that creep out during the night. Yet, I love him with all that is in me to love.

Several years ago, I remember ranting on and on about the incessant snoring while visiting my sweet elderly friend, Margie. She just smiled and said, "But you wouldn't give it up for anything would you?" I had to admit I wouldn't.

Then one day not long after I'd ranted and raved about his snoring, he stopped at a red light, turned his head, and momentarily went blind. Of course, it scared the yogurt out of him. And when he told me about it, I insisted that he contact our doctor who in turn sent him directly to the ER.

After hours upon hours of tests and waiting, the ER doc came in to tell us that he was calling in a neurologist and an oncologist. He said my husband either had a brain tumor or leukemia. To which my husband said, "So what's behind door number three?"

Time came to a screeching halt for my family. Nothing mattered to me except my husband. I was immediately transported in my mind to his funeral, crying hysterically at his coffin, begging God to just let me hear him snore one more time—just one more time. I'd even accept the gas.

Nothing prepared me, however, for the task of having to tell our children—all young adults at this time—who adored their father. Our oldest daughter, Sandi, lived in Georgia (and still does) with her husband and three kids. Our middle daughter, Noel, was just starting out on her own and at the beginning of her career. Our youngest daughter, Ashlee, was in college and working part-time. The daunting task of having to tell them lay before me, and all I wanted to do was to run and hide.

On this particular day, Noel and Ashlee were working together and had just stopped for lunch. I tracked them down and as I sat with them at the table, I reached out to God for the words. I have no idea what I said to them. My memory won't take me there. All I remember is it felt as though the air had been sucked right out of my lungs.

A brief silence, then Noel, always the rock, the glue that holds the sisters together, said, with her arm around Ashlee who had crumbled into a puddle of tears, "Do you want me to call Sandi?" I just nodded. And so she did. I'll admit to being totally useless at that point. Me, the mother. The one who should be the rock. Sandi didn't take it well. Her husband came home to find her in a fetal position in the middle of their bed crying uncontrollably, demanding, through her sobs, that he book a flight out to Dallas that instant. He did.

The next morning, we were all together standing around David's hospital bed. By this time more tests were in the works by the neurologist and the oncologist. The results brought the glorious news that he did not have a brain tumor or leukemia and that the initial tests, although they *had* indicated the possibility, really should not have been shared with us until more conclusive tests had been run. But that's a story for another day.

At that moment, the floodgates opened and all I could do was sob into my husband's chest. The girls were uncontrollable. Screaming and laughing and crying all at the same time. At one point I thought they might throw us out of the hospital. But none of us cared. We needed our celebration.

As for me, I don't complain as much about his snoring—or at least I try hard not to. Now we laugh about the creepy sneakers that invade our bed covers from time to time because we remember that day when life's imperfections took a backseat to the possibility of death.

On those times when his snoring is off the chain, I fall back in time to that day when I asked God to keep my husband forever snoring in my ear. And I thank Him for making us all beautifully imperfect.

Story #12

Marcia Brady...Women's Libber!

T̶HE WOMEN'S LIBERATION MOVEMENT. SOUNDS QUITE GRIM, I think. Especially when you look at the word *liberate—the setting free from bondage or prison.* I'm not sure I or my mother or even my grandmother ever felt bound or imprisoned. Not when we have always held the switch. Unbeknownst to most women libbers, we have ruled the world from the beginning of time. Take Eve for instance. Need I say more?

The mission of the *Movement* has eluded me for years, although as a teenager I longed to be a *Libber.* I even participated in a bra-burning protest. Of course, I had no idea what the protest signified. It just seemed cool at the time.

Feminism, by definition, is a doctrine whereby women are equal in every way to men. Kinda flies in the face of our Biblical teachings. It's a bit of a farce, however diligently the leaders of the women's lib try to make us believe it is a removal of attitudes and practices. The perception that men are superior to women is the fuel that feeds the fire of The Women's Liberation Movement.

The Brady Bunch came to televisions everywhere in 1969. It revolved around a large blended family made up of six kids, two parents, and a housekeeper. Originally the producer of the show wanted the mom to be a divorcee and the dad a widower. But, alas, the network said, "Ain't gonna happen." So they all decided the whereabouts of the mom's husband would be a mystery while we knew the dad to be a widower. Equality? I should say not! I'm sure that caused a multitude of bra burnings.

The Brady family sagas only revolved around softball topics with no meat—nothing to sink one's teeth into and gnaw over a bit. You didn't get all riled up and red-faced shaking your fist at the television vowing to never watch again. Bobby and Cindy were either feeling left out as the youngest siblings or getting in trouble for tattling. Jan saw the green jealousy monster every time she felt others were comparing her to her sister, Marcia. Peter couldn't decide if pimples, being boring or his voice changing were the most traumatic things in life. Greg just wanted his own room. Marcia found herself conflicted as to whether or not brushing her hair a hundred times really made it shine or not.

Then that fateful day arrived—the day The Women's Liberation Movement crept its way into the Brady household and left all the men wondering when and how Marcia became a Women's Libber!

It all began when a television news reporter showed up at Marcia's school. The topic of his report centered on how the women's liberation movement affected teenagers. Marcia made the mistake of answering the question honestly. From that point, the reporter turned her own words against her. Instead of making the case for equality, it negated her best point.

After the Brady boys watched the interview, it then became a contest. Greg turned into a sexist pig, and Marcia became determined to prove the point that a woman could do anything a man could do. She immediately petitioned to join Greg's Frontier Scouts which just so happened to be an organization made up of all males.

Greg did everything he could to cause Marcia to fail. To his dismay, he didn't succeed. Marcia passed them all, and the group had to accept her as a member.

After all the drama subsided and Greg had licked his wounds over Marcia's success, the story came full circle.

Although the general female audience most likely viewed it as a win for the *Movement,* I came away from it with a different slant. Equality by definition is broken down into several descriptions. One is sameness. Clearly, men and women are not the same physically or mentally. Just a fact.

Another description is ability. That is fodder for debate. It mostly centers around upper body strength. From what I've read, men have the edge in that regard, so it stands to reason there would be a shift in our ability when it comes to certain things. Some would argue that women can build upon their upper body. I would ask at what price? It does tend to mess with all that other female equipment.

Although Marcia Brady passed the tests required to become a Frontier Scout, she didn't accept the invitation to join. Why? She never wanted to be "the equal to boys in every way" as presented by the reporter. Instead, she just wanted the chance to try, which is the other definition of equality—fairness and impartiality.

It's no coincidence the good Lord made men and women different. His work is impeccable. "Wives, be subject to your husbands, as to the Lord. For the husband is the head of the wife, as Christ also is the head of the church, He Himself being the Savior of the body. But as the church is subject to Christ, so also the wives ought to be to their husbands in everything. Husbands, love your wives, just as Christ also loved the church and gave Himself for her" (Ephesians 5:22-25). Written by Paul, the woman-hater. Or that's what those who try to undermine God want us to believe. Within those verses is the beauty that lies within our differences and the love God intended a woman to have for a man and in return a man to have for a woman.

I've never really been a *Libber*. I'm too smart for that. Not a brag, just a fact. Truth be told, most women are too smart for that. We've learned the secret to catching flies. It helps when we want to be the boss. I'm sure most men, when speaking to relationships within a family, have seen what the boss's job looks like, and they most likely want no part of it. That's precisely why women have the babies. Only a boss could endure that kind of pain.

Personally, I like having doors opened and chairs pulled out. And if I smoked, I'd like my cigarette lit, too. Whatever happened to men standing when a woman enters the room? I can answer that. The Women's Liberation Movement.

I have never in my entire life been a frou-frou girl. I leaned far over to the side of a tomboy growing up. However, I never passed on an opportunity to play the damsel in distress. I don't mind being rescued. I rather enjoy being a woman and have no inclination to be otherwise. I love it when the knight in shining armor comes riding up to rescue his princess. And when they ride off together in the sunset.

Words like *de-sexing* muddle the brain and ties the tongue making certain words taboo. We find ourselves confused as to who the *she-men* and the *he-women* are. It's no wonder our young men and women of today don't know whether to scratch their watch or wind their butt, to coin a phrase. All the loveliness and strength that is a woman has been de-sexed. Just as men have had their masculinity whittled down to the point of making them nothing more than sniveling little mamas' boys.

From the beginning, Marcia Brady wanted what every woman wants—the chance to try. That doesn't strip a woman's femininity and turn them into women *Libbers*. It makes them equals—only not in every way. It liberates because we're given the chance. And on occasion, when we want to be, it also makes us the boss. Until we want to be rescued. That only takes a wink and a smile—guys fall for it every time.

Oh, and at the end of the show, I never did see any "Marcia Brady—Women's Libber" t-shirts for sale.

Story #13

Mothers, Daughters, High Heels, and Pearls

IT NEVER OCCURRED TO ME THAT HIGH HEELS AND PEARLS WOULD end up being the biggest contention between my mother and me—until now. I recently turned sixty-eight. Kind of a milestone. My mother, on the other hand, lived to be ninety-eight. Now that *is* a milestone. It's funny how we look back when we reach certain points in our lives. I find myself doing that looking back thing a lot lately.

My mother and I always had a different sort of relationship. She wanting me to do what she wanted me to do, and me wanting to do what I wanted to do. It rarely did either of us any good.

An only child, and a late-in-life child at that, my parents thought it prudent to enroll me in every activity known to man. Piano, dance, drama, and even etiquette class, just to name a few. Why not? Being a girl made me a prime candidate for these types of activities. Never mind that I hated girly things. It became my mother's mission in life to turn me into her dream of a mini-her. All high heels and pearls alongside that Southern lady's charm.

Upon discovering my outside voice and how to use it in ways to best embarrass my mother, I set out to make it humanly impossible for her to sway me to her way of thinking. Words my mother only spoke in a whisper, because it was unladylike to verbalize any other way, came in handy. I took great delight in using my newfound outside voice when repeating them in public.

Friday nights at our house meant candlelit family dinners. As an only child, you get included in this type of nonsense. My mother insisted on dressing for dinner, which for her included high heels and pearls. I don't think it mattered much about the event. She could be found most times in high heels and pearls. For the longest time, I believed my mother thought herself to be the real-life June Cleaver. But one particular Friday night, I showed up for dinner wearing a very ungirly shirt and corduroy pants. I call this—Exhibit A.

Let it never be said that my mother ever considered herself the underdog in our relationship. I knew with every rebellious step I took I came ever closer to the end of my young life. Mothers have a tipping point, you know.

As daughters, we find ourselves at war with our mothers throughout our growing up years. My mother and I spent many hours at war with each other. But when we do the looking back thing, we discover that was probably the best part of our life. We just didn't believe it while we were going through it.

I've never been prone to outbursts of emotion—crying uncontrollably at Kleenex tissue commercials and the like. It's never been a part of my makeup until I entered my sixties. I'm not sure if it's because of the looking back thing or leftover menopause, but I found I teared up a lot more often, which always made my mother happy. She considered it a small victory while she was still with me. She sometimes forgot my childhood days were behind me, but she still smiled when she noticed the mist in my eyes as she evilly twisted her pearls with her fingers.

Most people who knew my mother described her as a force to be reckoned with and the type one should never cross. Both true. Both good traits to have in your arsenal, especially when dealing with the likes of me. Consequently, it didn't take long for my mother to win the pearl throw-down. I believe it didn't come down to her powers of persuasion but her powers of bribery—a birthday party with as many kids as I wanted to invite held outside. The dress was her idea. I call this Exhibit B:

From that point on my mother pushed just a little harder with each passing year. I found myself being indoctrinated into this world of high heels and pearls. It mattered not my feelings on the subject. Mother had little concern that my guy friends who I played marbles with every weekend, might find this type of ensemble quite funny considering the fact that I could hold my own be it shooting marbles, climbing trees, foot races, or bike riding. My mother's ultimate goal—girly girl. The matching poses for the camera. And ultimately, the hats. I offer up Exhibits C and D respectively:

No wonder I rebelled! The gauntlet thrown down, I took it upon myself to solicit the aid of my outside voice. You see, the importance of not swallowing things—watermelon seeds, fingernails, dirt—were warnings I received regularly from my mother. She particularly warned me about swallowing watermelon seeds. According to her, a gigantic watermelon would grow inside my stomach if I continued this disgusting habit.

One Sunday evening I decided to get my revenge on my mother. Not only did I manage, on this particular day, to end her warnings of things growing inside my stomach, but I got a reprieve from her hounding me about all the necessary accessories and ensembles of a great Southern lady. It happened after prayer meeting during refreshment time, and it came in the form of a simple question directed at our preacher's wife, an exceptionally kind and plump woman.

Looking up at her with all the wide-eyed innocence I could muster I said, "How many watermelon seeds did you have to swallow to get that great big watermelon in your stomach?" Amazing how quickly a group of men can gather around a woman in high heels and pearls after she has fainted dead away on the floor. It's also interesting how a bar of soap in one's mouth can have a sobering effect on a loud personality.

Sometimes we find ourselves wondering what it would be like if our mothers weren't around. And before we know it, they're not. It makes sense we should attempt to cherish the times we have together. I can't help wondering, however, how we ever survive each other's personalities.

My small victory in the battle of the high heels and pearls conflict is that I never succumbed to the pressure of wearing high heels. My mother, on the other hand, could no longer wear them in her old age. Sweet revenge for my side? Not really. She loved wearing high heels but when physical ailments prevented her from wearing something that gave her such pleasure, the ugly face of revenge took a back seat. But I'll tell you a little secret. I do, from time to time, wear pearls. I'll give her that victory. She earned it.

Story #14

Mr. Wolf

MY GRANDDAUGHTER HAS ABOUT A MILLION STUFFED ANIMALS. She has named them all. Three of them in particular are: an owl, named appropriately Mr. Owl, a dog named George, and a koala bear named Bert. They are her best friends. So one might assume by the title of this story that it could be about a wolf named Mr. Wolf. It could be. But it's not.

Mr. Wolf (spelled like the animal) lived next door to me when I was a little girl. I loved him like an uncle. He would visit us several times a week. I loved his visits. We'd play kickball in my backyard. We'd play checkers on the porch. My mother would fix us all some lemonade and cookies. But the best part about Mr. Wolf's visits were the stories he told.

I could never figure out how he knew so many stories. He said because he'd lived a long, long time. Most of the stories he told had animals in them as the main characters. I loved those the best. Once he told me about this wolf who lived in the woods out by his father's farm. I wondered if that was why his name was Mr. Wolf, but no, it just made the story better. Mr. Wolf said that wolves were extremely intelligent. That's why they had such a hard time trying to capture the wolf.

This wolf seemed different from other wolves because most wolves travel in packs. Mr. Wolf said he couldn't believe that this wolf traveled and hunted alone. And it seemed the thing he liked most were the chickens that lived on Mr. Wolf's father's farm. It took a long time to figure out how to catch the wolf. Mr. Wolf said that his daddy didn't want to hurt the wolf. Of course, that made me very happy.

"You see," said Mr. Wolf, "there's no way you can ever fool a wolf's nose. No sir, wolves have the best smellers there is. If they even catch a hint of a smell of a human they won't come anywhere near your trap. Their noses are so good that if you get even a drop of sweat on that trap you can kiss that wolf goodbye. Well, my daddy just couldn't see his way to trapping that wolf. But he had to find a way to keep the wolf from killing our chickens. Now you're not going to believe this, but my daddy decided he would find a wife for that old wolf. Don't laugh it's true. He found a man in our town who raised wolves. My daddy asked the man if he wouldn't mind bringing over one of his female wolves to our farm. The man agreed. As soon as those two wolves' eyes met, they fell madly in love. It's a known fact that wolves who fall in love stay together forever. Kinda like when Mrs. Wolf and I fell in love and got married. We promised to stay together for better or worse and through sickness and health until death do us part. Well, I could tell right away that those two wolves were meant for each other."

My eyes were bigger than saucers the entire time Mr. Wolf was telling the story. I asked, "Did they just go off into the sunset like cowboys do?"

Mr. Wolf laughed and said, "No, our wolf just followed his new love right into the cage the man brought with him when he brought the female wolf. You should've seen it. After that our chickens were safe, and those two wolves lived happily ever after."

Now I'm sure most of Mr. Wolf's stories were either tall tales or fables. All I know is that I loved listening to them.

At the age of about 8, I developed chickenpox. They now have a vaccine for it that kids receive between twelve and fifteen months and again between four and six years. In 1960, the vaccine didn't exist and I came down with a grand case of

If the Story Fits Tell It

it. From the time I contracted it my life consisted of oatmeal baths and the overabundant application of calamine lotion. Scratching is the problem, so my mother put gloves on me. Then there's the fever that goes with it all.

What upset me the most had nothing to do with the actual chickenpox. The fact that chickenpox is so contagious meant I couldn't see Mr. Wolf. I couldn't play kickball with him, and I couldn't listen to his stories. When you have chickenpox, you're contagious from the beginning until the lesions crust or scab over.

When Mr. Wolf heard about the chickenpox, he came right over. You must remember we were living in 1960 and the vaccine didn't come around until 1995. Plus, chickenpox is an airborne disease that spreads easily through the coughs and sneezes of an infected person. These tidbits of info weren't known at the time. So Mr. Wolf thought nothing of just popping over to check on me. He brought me a stuffed animal. A wolf, of course. I couldn't have been happier to see him, and I immediately named the stuffed animal Mr. Wolf.

Several days later, my mother received a phone call that Mr. Wolf had the chickenpox. It was serious. When you're older, like Mr. Wolf was, chickenpox becomes more severe. Mr. Wolf didn't realize he'd never had chickenpox as a child. Adults can develop severe pneumonia and other serious complications. Mr. Wolf was very sick. It broke my heart.

Mr. Wolf had gotten the chickenpox from me. I remember crying and crying and crying. My mother couldn't console me. I knew Mr. Wolf could die. What would I do then? How could I ever make it up to Mrs. Wolf? She would never forgive me. I think I prayed non-stop for days.

Mr. Wolf didn't die. He came through it, but it took a lot

longer for him than it did for me. I asked my mother every day if I could go visit him like he visited me. The answer always came back, no.

When they finally let me see Mr. Wolf, I ran as fast as I could over to his house. As I walked through the door, there sat Mr. Wolf in his favorite chair. He still had a couple of spots on his face but other than that he looked great.

He greeted me with a big smile on his face and said, "Did I ever tell you the story about…"

Story #15

My Mother's Hands

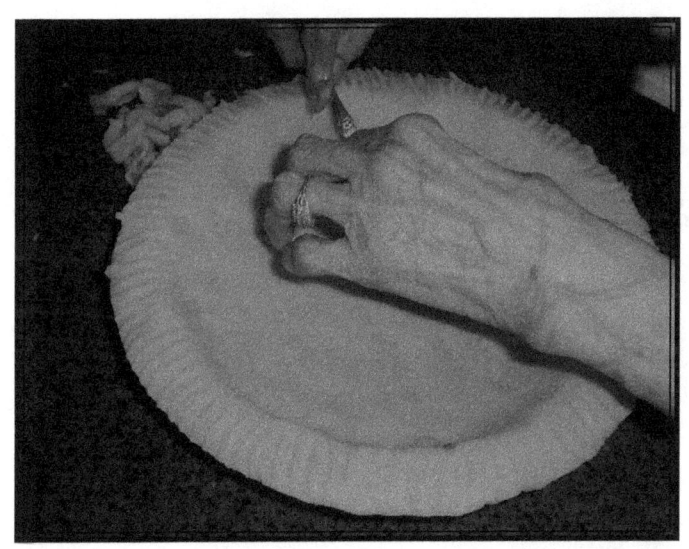

I DON'T REMEMBER WHEN I NOTICED THAT MY HANDS WERE beginning to look like my mother's. I'm sure it had to have been one of those days when time stood still. You know, the kind when there's nothing else to do but look at your hands. I remember becoming distressed over it. My hands were taking on all the characteristics of my mother's.

It would be glorious if my mother's hands were beautiful, but they weren't. They never were. Even as a kid I noticed my mother's hands were boney. Never manicured. She didn't bite her nails, but she never painted them either. I couldn't understand the no painting part because all my friends' mothers had painted nails.

I hated it when my mother would point at me with those ugly, boney fingers of hers. Suddenly, she took on the appearance of one of those wicked witches I read about in scary books. Looking back on that I really *do* feel bad that I felt that way, because my mother never looked like a witch. She was always quite lovely. It was just her hands! There are so many beautiful hands in the world. There are even people who model just their hands. My mother never could have done that. Some people even insure their hands.

What are some of the ways we can use our hands? Let's make a list!

1. Clap
2. Eat
3. Work—that alone encompasses millions of things
4. Pat our animals on the head as well as our children
5. Bathe or shower
6. Put on our clothes, our socks, our shoes
7. Comb or brush our hair

8. Wave hello and goodbye
9. Write
10. Play a musical instrument
11. Use sign language

This is just a short list, but there are many more things we do with our hands. Did you know the Bible speaks to hands? The word *hand* appears in the Bible. How many times you ask? How about 1,466 times. Seriously, yes. That's not all. The word *hands* appears in the Bible 462 times. Thought you'd like to know that bit of trivia, just in case.

So, I'm looking at my hands this one day I can't remember and I notice I'm going to have my mother's hands in the not too distant future. Then I start thinking seriously about my mother's hands. Not just their appearance, but what they did during her lifetime.

She used those hands for the main reason God gave them to her—to pray. You'll notice that God didn't give us just one hand He gave us two. They help one another. They pull those we love close to us. But my mother used her hands for so many things that benefited me. Had I actually forgotten about that? She used them to ride a camel, too, but we won't go there now.

An amazing seamstress, my mother made my clothes until I started high school. After that, I became too snooty for handmade clothes. Imagine that—a snooty teen. She started back up again making clothes when my three girls were born. She made each one of them three dresses a year: one for their birthday, one for Easter, and one for Christmas. It never failed to be a true labor of love.

My mother's sewing talent aided in the making of curtains, costumes, all manner of fancy napkins, quilts, even shirts for my daddy. She made pillowcases, mended clothing, and made baby clothes for many families.

She wasn't the best cook in the world, especially since my daddy was a chef, but there were some things in which she outdid him. Things like banana pudding, chicken and pastries, peach cobbler, fried chicken, and my favorite, minced meat pie, which she made for me every Christmas until she passed away.

She helped me with my piano lessons, something I had to take as an extension of my physical therapy after hand surgery. I began taking piano at the age of nine. I hated it, but not for any other reason than it hurt the hand that required the surgery and therapy. My teacher, Mrs. Clarey, couldn't have been more wonderful. She and my mother became close friends. When Mrs. Clarey discovered my mother could play the piano, she asked her to help with practice. Mother agreed. Over time it became easier and I eventually came to love playing the piano.

My parents were never wealthy. Never poor either. They lived quite comfortably. My daddy grew up an only child and never really wanted for anything. My mother's family housed twelve kids. They lived on a farm. Grew and raised all their food. Her daddy also did carpentry work. They lived through the depression, but it never really touched them. Likewise, as an only child, I never wanted for anything either. My parents never lived outside their means. They took advantage of their abilities to make way for other things they liked to do and have.

Since my mother taught school before I invaded her world, I never lacked for help with schoolwork or school projects. My lunch box always contained nutritious meals. I always had a snack waiting for me when I came home from school.

An avid reader, my mother made sure I had access to as many books as possible. On those days when the weather made it impossible to go outside, my mother would sit with me and we'd read together. I enjoyed listening to her read but never really enjoyed reading myself. She knew this and slowly brought me around to the joy of reading.

Birthday parties were huge in my family. Since my daddy's birthday was May 20th and my birthday, May 22nd, on May 21st we celebrated both our birthdays with my mother planning a party and making a cake for us to share.

At night, there'd be a bedtime story, a goodnight prayer, and mother's hands on my face as she kissed me goodnight. Those boney hands. Those hands I saw that day I don't remember when I found myself looking at my own hands in dismay.

All the times she held my face or my hand or tucked me in bed or bandaged a knee or disciplined me—all those everyday deeds, all those hours spent doing multiple things, things I'm sure I took for granted, helping me, helping my daddy, helping others—they were all accomplished—every one of them—with my mother's hands.

Story #16

Pardon Me, But I Think I've Lost My Way to Sesame Street

Since I was born in 1952, seventeen years before the premiere of *Sesame Street*, I did not have the advantages afforded later generations of this popular show. It has always seemed odd to me that a program known for its educational content, coupled with its knack for communication, would always be asking how to get there. Don't get me wrong, I like *Sesame Street*. Children have loved *Sesame Street* since 1969. It's a great show, a great place—if only you could find it. Following the big yellow bird seemed the most appropriate way to discover its location.

On those times in my own life when I've found myself lost, my mind does tend to ask the way to *Sesame Street*. I mean, there are friendly neighbors there, happy people, every door is open, and the air is sweet. What could be more perfect? Heaven maybe? Although I do look forward to Heaven, I'm not quite ready to go there yet. I have visions of seeing my granddaughter, Skye, sworn in as the first woman President of the United States. Then there's my grandson, Dylan, who is destined to take over the computer industry. My granddaughter, Danielle, will certainly discover the cure for some dreaded disease. My granddaughter, Haylie, will surely become famous in some way, be it art, acting, dancing, or storytelling. Then there's my granddaughter, Finley. Too young yet to predict, but I know she will be magnificent in whatever she's called to do. I need to be around to see all these things happen.

So maybe I should just focus on trying to find *Sesame Street* within myself. With the dawn of too many New Years, however, I've found myself a bit deflated. Not wanting to celebrate the usual resolutions towards a better year or a better life or even a better body.

My minister put it this way one Sunday—let us each celebrate the New Year's *revolution*. Jesus, he said, was a revolutionary, not a resolutionary. My Church, The United Methodist Church, was founded on "The Covenant Prayer" by John Wesley that takes a revolutionary stand on who we belong to as people. When I hear words like "I am no longer my own, but thine," and "Put me to what thou wilt, rank me with whom thou wilt," and especially "Put me to doing," read out loud, they sometimes ring hollow. Especially the *doing* part, because I've been *doing* for crying out loud! Sorry about that bit of a tantrum.

Truth be known, my minister tends to nudge me a bit. No, actually he's been known to poke me exceptionally hard. It annoys me. I've never told him this because I really like him, and it would probably hurt his feelings. They talk about feelings a lot on *Sesame Street*—wherever that is.

I remember his sermon series a couple of years ago on *It's a Wonderful Life,* only he called it *It's a Wonder-Full Life.* He's a big play-on-words kind of guy. My family happened to be going through a scary time, and I just wasn't in the mood to hear about George Bailey (whom I hated anyway). You can only watch that movie a thousand times before you're shouting, "ENOUGH ALREADY!" Maybe George knows the way to *Sesame Street.*

So, the New Year came and went and my resolution list lay empty. I hadn't even started a revolution list which made me feel even worse. Obviously, I must be lost. I'm usually on top of stuff like this. But right now I have no map and the road to that place isn't marked clearly enough, so how could I even begin to make lists of anything—resolutionary, revolutionary, or otherwise? Everything is definitely not "A-OK."

If the Story Fits Tell It

I'm tired. Tired of trying. Tired of pushing. Tired of hitting one brick wall after another. Tired of having doors shut in my face or worse being ignored. And I'm particularly tired of not being able to find the way to *Sesame Street*. I think I've at least earned some sort of magic carpet ride to a place where there are happy people like me.

Other parts of "The Covenant Prayer" didn't make me any happier either. "Let me be full, let me be empty. Let me have all things, let me have nothing. Put me to suffering." I began to wonder if John Wesley might have been lost himself. He was just a man, after all, who lived a really long time ago. The 1700s to be exact. What could he possibly have known about the direction the world would go? The pressures, the stresses, the twenty-four-seven news cycle, the economy, the price of food and gas, the corruption, the violence—and the lack of maps that lead to *Sesame Street*!

I doubt I'll ever find that place where the air is sweet. Not here on earth anyway. Maybe that's why they keep asking the way. Maybe that's why there is no map. Maybe my wanting to go there is not where God wants me to go, but I want to go there anyway. I want to find that place because it sounds magical. Nothing will be expected of me there. I can just stop. No pressures, no stresses, no anything—just open doors and happy people everywhere.

The last part of "The Covenant Prayer" is the biggest challenge, and it is most likely the reason the location to *Sesame Street* remains so mysterious. "I freely and heartily yield all things to thy pleasure and disposal." That would take some courage, would it not? Man, that's tough. It's most likely the reason "The Covenant Prayer" flies in my face. Courage has never been my middle name.

The New Year brought with it a double-dog dare that sucked the wind right out of my lungs. "Remember I (God) commanded you to be strong and brave. Don't be afraid, because the Lord your God will be with you wherever you go." Joshua 1:9—my New Year's Day Bible verse. And the Lord said, "Gotcha!" I became annoyed all over again.

I now find myself in a tug of war—me pulling in one direction and the Lord pulling in the other. And *Sesame Street* is nowhere in sight. The only thing I see is the "The Covenant Prayer" filled with all these challenges I don't want to take. I'm shamed by the words, "And now, O glorious and blessed God, Father, Son, and Holy Spirit, thou art mine, and I am thine." I don't feel worthy.

In my dreams, I see myself wandering down this road unfamiliar to me, walking up to perfect strangers and asking for directions to the place I want to be. No one seems to know.

"Can you tell me how to get to *Sesame Street*?"

"I SAY! Can you tell me how to get to *Sesame Street*?"

"PARDON ME, BUT I THINK I'VE LOST MY WAY TO SESAME STREET!" Suddenly I wake up.

The Lord whispers in my ear, "You are *Mine,* and I am yours."

I sigh, then take in some air. It's strange, but for some reason, the air seems sweet. "And the covenant which I have made on earth, Let it be ratified in Heaven." So be it.

The moral? Who needs *Sesame Street* anyway?

Story #17

The Difference Between Peggy and Aunt Virginia

I CAN'T HELP BUT SMILE WHEN I THINK OF PEGGY. A FRIEND FIRST, my family's maid second. I grew up with Peggy around. My mother hired her away from another family. She did all the cleaning, washing, ironing, and some light cooking. She also scolded me when I did something wrong. And, depending on how bad the wrong I'd done, she even spanked me.

My parents were big advocates of doing the best you could at any task—something they instilled in me. Daddy always said if digging ditches happened to be the only job available to him to support his family, he'd be the best dang ditch digger known to mankind. Anyone my parents hired to do a job were the best at that job, regardless of who they might be. They always looked for people who took pride in their work. Peggy was the best of the best.

When Peggy first started working for us, she had no idea that the color of her skin meant nothing to us. Mother hired her because her abilities as a maid were excellent. Peggy, on the other hand, saw herself only as our maid. A black woman working for a white family. Only we weren't white, exactly. We are mostly Cherokee. There might be a little white along the way but not so you'd notice. Still, Peggy saw us as white.

The day she discovered we had no aversion to the color of her skin happened one day when my daddy drove Peggy home. She'd been working for us for about a month. Her daughter typically came to pick her up. On this one day, her daughter couldn't get off work in time to get to our house. Peggy asked my daddy if he would take her home.

"Of course," Daddy said.

As they approached the car, Peggy walked over to the back-seat door on the passenger side.

"What are you doing?" asked Daddy.

Peggy looked confused. "I'm gettin' in the car, Mr. Claude," she answered.

"You don't need to get in the back seat, Peggy. Sit up front with me."

"Why, Mr. Claude, that wouldn't be right," said Peggy.

"And why not?" asked Daddy.

"Mr. Claude, you're my boss. I work for you. You're a white man. I'm a black woman. It ain't proper. What would people think me ridin' up front with you?"

"It's my car isn't it?" asked Daddy.

"Yes, sir, it is," Peggy answered.

"Look, Peggy, it makes no difference to me what people think or say. You are a part of our family. We have grown to love and respect you. Evelyn and Regina adore you, as I do. We don't think of you any other way. Don't you know that?"

Peggy wiped a tear from her eye and said, "Mr. Claude, I guess I always felt that, but I never wanted you to think I was too big for my britches by just gettin' in the front seat. I would never do anything to make people talk."

My daddy laughed and said, "Peggy, I'm about 6'2" tall. I weigh about 240 pounds. Who do you think is going to mess with me?"

They both laughed and laughed. Then Daddy walked around the car and opened the front door to the passenger's side and said, "Now get in this car, Peggy!"

"Yes, sir, Mr. Claude!" said Peggy with a smile.

From that moment on Peggy never questioned how we felt about her. She knew we loved her. She worked for us for several years before she had to retire due to her health. I find it amusing that people who tend to look down on those who work for them in a housekeeping capacity, especially if the housekeeper is black, have no problems with them disciplining their children. I grew up a child of the 50s and 60s, a time when racism had its grip. Nevertheless, black maids could whip the livin' daylights out of the white kids.

I've always believed that the reason my family held different views came from not only because we believed racism to be wrong but because we, too, faced prejudices and racism being from a Cherokee Indian heritage. All one needs to do is some research on the 1830 Congress. The same year that Congress passed the Indian Removal Act. Then in 1838/39 the state of Georgia prompted or instructed U.S. troops to remove the Cherokee from their ancestral homeland. Sending them to what we know now as Oklahoma. But, I digress.

When we heard the news of Peggy's passing, we reached out to her daughter, and she welcomed us into her home as we paid our last respects to our dear friend. Peggy will remain in my memory as a woman of dignity and grace.

My Aunt Virginia also left an impression on me I'll not soon forget. Like Peggy, I loved her dearly. Unlike Peggy, my Aunt Virginia utilized her strong will. However, she wasn't always like that. In her earlier years, she felt unworthy of respect. This low self-esteem had nothing to do with society. It had to do with the fact that her husband abused her. As a small child, I have memories of the abuse my Aunt Virginia took at the hands of her husband. I didn't understand it, of course. All I knew was that it scared me.

Then, through a turn of events that might have pushed her over the edge into self-degradation, those tragic events ultimately provided her with a springboard that catapulted her to self-worth. From that point on, she never allowed anyone, even though she came from a long line of Cherokee and Lumbee Indians, to look down on her or disrespect her in any way. I always admired her tenacity. She was a force.

The summers I spent with my grandparents allowed me to visit with Aunt Virginia. By this time, she and her husband had experienced a reckoning. He no longer held the key to her self-worth. The transformation in him could only be described as remarkable. God stepped right in the middle of that marriage and made it whole. Aunt Virginia became her own woman.

When Aunt Virginia invited me over to her house to spend the night, well, let's just say silliness showed up. I loved going through her closet and looking at all her beautiful clothes. She would turn on the radio so we could listen to her favorite artist, Conway Twitty.

Aunt Virginia loved Elvis Presley, too. You know, some say he and Conway Twitty sounded alike. Maybe that's why she loved them both. If there was an Elvis Presley movie playing at the local theater during my visits, she'd take me. The movie, however, is not what has stayed with me all these years. When you walked into the theater after purchasing your ticket, there stood two signs. One read: *Coloreds sit in the back.* The other read: *Indians sit in the balcony.* I didn't understand. My Aunt Virginia told me, "Don't mind those. I love sittin' in the balcony. You can see the whole screen from up there. You'll see. You're gonna love it too."

But I didn't love it. Oh, you could see the entire screen alright. You just didn't have the freedom to choose where in the theater *you* wanted to sit. Aunt Virginia did her best to wash over it, pretending it didn't matter. That, in fact, the rule of having to sit in the balcony if you were Indian had backfired because, from her point of view, it was the best seat in the house. You could see everything.

Peggy and Aunt Virginia. Two minority women who looked different on the outside but shared the same vulnerabilities on the inside. Two women who came into my life and made a difference in how I view freedom, in how I view womanhood, in how I view the meaning of respect. I loved them both equally. I miss them both still.

Story #18

Redneckness Must Be a Disease

After many years of marriage, one might think I would know I married a redneck. But it tends to sneak up on me because he never appeared as a full-blown redneck. You know, the kind that drives a truck with a gun rack in the window or camper on the back? Or the ones with bumper stickers that read, "Keep Honkin' I'm reloadin'" or "Mess with me and you mess with the whole trailer park." You know those kinds of rednecks, right? My husband has never done any of that. There's something to be said for the whole denial thing.

Okay, so he does drive a truck, but he certainly doesn't have those disgusting mud flaps with the scantily clad women on them. Okay, so he watches *Moonshiners* and *Swamp People* and *Turtle Man* and *American Hoggers*. Everyone knows these are all harmless pastimes. But I put my foot down when it came to *Pit Bulls and Parolees*. Have you seen those people?

In the beginning, he only attempted little redneck things. Like the time our console television went out. He bought us a new portable one and proceeded to put the new television on top of the broken television. This was long before the big screen T.V. we see now in every household around America. Or the time he put aluminum foil in our apartment windows. He claimed it would help with the utility bills. There were other things, but I'm too much of a lady to mention them.

Now for the cold hard truth. Over the years, I admit I've sat idly by and watched as the man I took those lifelong vows with many years ago has steadily emerged into a full-blown redneck of gigantic proportions.

What finally brought me to this eye-opening revelation? I walked outside one day only to discover that my partner in life, my husband, the father of my children, had turned our back yard into a drive-by redneck boiled peanut stand. Where had I gone wrong? It suddenly became clear. I couldn't be a bystander any longer. I needed to make arrangements for an intervention. Time had come to call in the big guns. I knew this person, more than anyone, would know what to do. I mean this dude wrote the book on rednecks.

I snapped a picture, not only for posterity but as proof to the intervenor that my husband was indeed suffering from the disease known as Redneckness. With evidence in hand, I ran to my computer and wrote to the one person I knew could help:

Dear Jeff Foxworthy: You know you're married to a redneck when he hooks up the propane tank to a pot and proceeds to boil peanuts in the backyard. Who does this? Help!

Kindest regards, your friend, Regina

I knew this would be the answer to my dilemma. I mean, I couldn't stand idly by and watch my husband turn into a redneck of gigantic proportions. Didn't I say the words at the altar on our wedding day, "In sickness and in health." Didn't I promise to stand by my man?

I waited patiently for the response. Finally, it came.

Dear Regina: That is a great idea! Best wishes, your fellow redneck, Jeff Foxworthy

Not the answer I had hoped for. "Fellow redneck" indeed! I couldn't have been more disappointed. And at that moment it occurred to me—these rednecks stick together.

Distraught and disillusioned, I searched for answers as to why I hadn't noticed this slow but progressive redness crawling up the back of my husband's neck. He certainly didn't come from a redneck family. His parents were humble people who would have never been seen behaving in such a manner. His siblings always seemed normal, sorta. The neighborhood he grew up in always appeared to be a redneck free zone. So what happened to cause my husband to turn into this backyard, peanut boiling, redneck crazy person? We may never know.

I finally resolved within myself that I had no choice but to accept the distasteful fact that my husband had slowly, over the years of our marriage, turned into a full-blown, Jeff Foxworthy, card totin' redneck. For better or worse, I kept reminding myself. In sickness and in health. That's the one! The vow that explains everything. Because everyone knows redneckness *must* be a disease.

Story #19

Superfluous Buns

Up until the time I saw the movie *Father of the Bride*, the only superfluous buns I knew about were my own due to eating too many peanut M&M's. But when I heard George Banks' well-written rant, I knew the word superfluous had a far-reaching meaning and significance.

The 1991 remake of the 1950 film features as its main character, the loveable George Banks. George goes over the edge one day in a supermarket over hot dog buns, and it all stems from his daughter's upcoming wedding. The rant he unleashes on the poor, unsuspecting stock boy made me stand up and cheer.

George couldn't understand why, if he only wanted eight hot dog buns, he had to pay for twelve. Hot dogs come in packages of eight. In the movie, no one sold eight hot dog buns. They only sold twelve. George then proceeds to remove the *superfluous* buns. The stock boy becomes quite concerned at this point, but George explains his version of why he's forced to pay for something he doesn't need. It's the fault of the big-shots at the wiener company and the big-shots at the bun company. According to George, they were in cahoots together, ripping off the American public. Why would they do this? Because they think we're a bunch of nit-wits. We're so trusting, we'd pay for anything. Even things we don't need. Just because we don't want to make a stink over anything. Well, George is having none of it. He makes a stink. He's not paying for anything he doesn't need ever again! And with that, he promptly goes to jail.

Thankfully, none of us will suffer from having to buy more hot dog buns than we need. Thanks to George Banks, who started the hot dog bun movement, we can now purchase eight hot dog buns. Let's hear it for George!

I started thinking about the word superfluous and its meaning. It's a good word. It occurred to me that the American public *does* buy into it. We *are* a bunch of nitwits, often because we enjoy being excessive. It makes us feel important. We spend millions of dollars on needless items. Extravagant items. Unnecessary items. We use those items to fill the holes in our lives.

At the beginning of the movie *Places in the Heart,* short-lived character Royce Spalding said grace over the Sunday meal. I thought it significant and have always remembered it. He prays, "Make us thankful for Your generous bounty, and Your unceasing love. Please remind us, in these hard times, to be grateful for what we have been given, and not to ask for what we cannot have." But we do ask—all the time. We do want the superfluous buns. I submit we want an overabundance of superfluous buns. Is that not the definition of entitlement? Greed? Self-indulgence? Even gluttony? By the way, Royce Spalding fell victim to a gunshot wound to the chest—just in case you were wondering why he didn't last out the movie as he seemed so wise.

My parents never wanted me to come across as an only child. Even though I always felt it to be their fault I had no siblings, they were intent on proving that an only child didn't have to be a brat. Parents of only children weren't *required* to spoil their child with an abundance of superfluous buns; it just always seemed to turn out that way. Maybe because they actually felt sorry for the kid.

I never had a room full of toys or even my own car as a teen. My mother made my clothes for most of my growing-up years. I didn't even get an allowance. My parents didn't believe in allowances. They didn't believe in giving children money to do the things they were supposed to do in the first place. I had chores. There were certain things my parents expected of me. In return, they allowed me to live. I did have my own bedroom. There were times, however, that I feared my parents might take it upon themselves to rent a kid to share my room to defend themselves for not having more kids.

My mother came from a family of fourteen (12 kids/2 parents) and my daddy from a family of three (1 kid/2 parents). From what I know of my paternal grandmother, she leaned to the side of the superfluous buns when it came to my daddy. My maternal grandparents, however, never missed a chance to impress upon their twelve children who ran the zoo. No superfluous buns allowed in their home.

As I reflected on George Banks' heartfelt message to an uncaring stock boy who only wanted him to stop pulling out the superfluous buns, I realized I, too, am guilty of being a nitwit. Wanting more of what I know I can't have. Scratching just below the surface of greed. I tend to pay for things I don't need. For what? I've asked myself that question a million times and I always answer it the same way. "I don't know. I just want it." Sad, sad, sad, and pitiful.

It doesn't end with individuals. We see this compulsion to pay for things we don't need in other areas—corporations, governments, and churches all grab for the superfluous buns. I wonder just how many of us can truthfully claim to be content with what we have. My guess is few, if any. We are the epitome of the big-shot wiener guys and the big-shot bun guys. Those superfluous buns bring us comfort. Oh, we'd never admit it mind you. But being content in what we have just ain't in our makeup. Need I mention Adam and Eve?

I once knew a lady who came close to being one of those people who found herself content in what she had. She qualified for "Meals on Wheels" but turned it down. She pointed to those who had less than she. Grateful for what she did have. I doubt she ever paid for anything she didn't need.

The Bible is clear regarding greed, gluttony, possessions, hoarding, and yes, superfluous buns. Matthew 6:19-21 reads, "Do not lay up for yourselves treasures on earth, where moth and rust destroy and where thieves break in and steal, but lay up for yourselves treasures in heaven, where neither moth nor rust destroys and where thieves do not break in and steal. For where your treasure is, there your heart will be also."

It's true. Our treasures always find their way to our hearts. And although George Banks had had enough of paying for things he didn't need, many of us will continue to pay for the superfluous buns. I'm thinking if I would just cut out the peanut M&M's my superfluous buns would disappear!

Story #20

The Corncob Pipe in Daddy's Pipe Stand

There's a legend surrounding the corncob pipe. Like most legends, there's a bit of truth and a bit of made-up stuff. The beginning of the corncob pipe is just such a story, or legend, if you will. It's one that has been passed down, from person to person, through time.

According to the legend of the corncob pipe, there lived this farmer who, for whatever reason, decided he'd take a corncob and whittle it down until he made a pipe. Well, he loved this pipe. It made him happy. He loved it so much he went in search of someone who might help him make another one, or even several.

Nearby lived a guy by the name of Henry Tibbe. Mr. Tibbe came from Holland. He and his family emigrated to the United States somewhere around the 1860s. Mr. Tibbe was a woodturner. A mighty good one at that. When he and his family finally settled in Missouri, Mr. Tibbe set up a woodworking business. Quite small at first, as most businesses are.

Now the farmer heard about Mr. Tibbe and sought him out. He showed Mr. Tibbe his corncob pipe and asked if he could help make more. Mr. Tibbe studied it for a moment, then he bored out the pith of a regular old corncob. Then he cut it in two. After that, he simply smoothed it out on his lathe, which he operated by foot-power. Finally, he inserted a reed that acted as a stem. The farmer loved it. Mr. Tibbe had created a much-improved version of the farmer's corncob pipe, and did it much more quickly. As a bonus, it looked just like a traditional knife whittled corncob pipe! And, the rest, as they say, is history.

If you remember, even Frosty the Snowman had a

corncob pipe. As did U.S. General Douglas MacArthur. Pretty famous people enjoyed the look and feel of a corncob pipe. Mark Twain also enjoyed smoking his corncob pipe from his native state of Connecticut.

My daddy owned such a pipe. Although he had quite a collection of pipes, I loved that corncob pipe the most. He often caught me playing with it, which didn't make him very happy. He'd give me the look, and I'd immediately return the pipe to its place in the pipe stand. The smells that came from those pipes are still fresh in my mind. If I think about them hard enough, I can literally catch a whiff of their fragrance. Sadly, all my daddy's pipes and pipe stand were lost when they moved out of their mountain home and back to Atlanta.

As for the rest of my family, the Morgans, who represented my Grandma Ella's family—that would be my daddy's mother—they were all Cherokee Indians. One of our family members wrote a book entitled *A Morgan Family Storybook*. It contained personal stories and biographical sketches told by the descendants of Squire James and Sarah Morgan from Transylvania County, North Carolina. The Morgans would gather annually in Brevard, North Carolina for a huge family reunion.

I loved going to these reunions in the mountains of Brevard, North Carolina, in an area made just for family reunions. The covered patio stood among the most magnificent trees. All the elders sat around the patio. No matter the weather, be it hot or cold, they all wore woolen mantles. And the men? Well, they were smoking corncob pipes. Oh yes!

The corncob pipe that stood in my daddy's pipe stand did not belong to his father, as his father came from Irish descent. Nope, it belonged to my daddy's grandfather, Squire

If the Story Fits Tell It

Andrew Morgan. To this day it makes me sick to know that my great-grandfather's corncob pipe mysteriously disappeared during my parents' move to Atlanta.

One Halloween, when my middle daughter was about three, we dressed her up in overalls and put a cowgirl hat on her. My daddy decided she needed a corncob pipe and proceeded to make her one. Now I'm not so sure it looked exactly like the corncob pipe that stood in my daddy's pipe stand, but according to my daddy, it looked pretty stinkin' close.

If I had a moral to this story, I'd say it might be:

Hold on to those good old things. Pay attention to the detail in their makeup. Be mindful of the legend surrounding them and pass that history down to your children and your grandchildren, whether they want to hear it or not. Because one day they, too, will look back and cherish the legend.

Story #21

The Day the Handshake Died

Photo by U.S. Army Signal Corps

*E*VER THINK OF THE HANDSHAKE AS A SHAKEDOWN? THAT shaking a person's hand means you're checking to make sure they don't have a weapon hidden somewhere in their hand or on their body? It's absolutely true. Well, maybe it was true a long time ago. Like in the 5th century B.C. We're talking medieval times. Oh yes, not only did the handshake signify peace, it also aided in making sure there were no concealed weapons. As one person approached another, if they both stuck out their hand that meant they came in peace—no weapons. Kinda like the aliens my husband believes in. After a while, the Romans decided they'd just grab one another's arm when meeting up. Don't know why. It just seemed appropriate, I guess.

Shakespeare mentions the handshake in *Julius Caesar* and in *As You Like It*. Even before the era of Shakespeare, Homer wrote about the handshake in *The Iliad*, when two of his characters shook hands certifying and pledging their faith to one another.

Being from the South, I've always thought of the handshake as a gentlemanly thing. Two men meeting up would always shake one another's hand. But a gentleman would never reach out first to shake a lady's hand. Oh no. That would be uncouth. A gentleman always waited to see if the lady extended her hand first before ever extending his. I'm pretty sure with the introduction of the Women's Liberation Movement in the late 1960s whether a man extended his hand first or not made very little difference and fell by the wayside. Women wanted nothing to do with gentlemen. I know this to be true since I grew up during that time. I didn't much like it then and don't much like it now.

Nevermind the WLM, my parents taught me that I should always offer my hand to a gentleman. It seemed fitting to me. The only time a gentleman held out his hand to a lady happened when he might be assisting her. For instance, during the days of my grandparents, it would be helping her in and out of a carriage. During the days of my parents, it would be the car as it still should be today. My husband has always held out his hand to assist me whether it be from the car or down a flight of stairs or walking across the street.

If you ask any of my girls they'll tell you that their daddy has always instructed them that any man who is not willing to hold out his hand in assistance isn't worth the time of day. He's also taught them that they should always offer their hand out when meeting someone for the first time—regardless of whether that person is male or female. And they always have.

Think of other reasons for the handshake. For years, the handshake came at the end of a business deal. Further back, it represented a man's word—his bond. Some business deals ended in agreement with a simple handshake. No papers required. When two people shook hands on a deal, that deal was sealed. The handshake has mostly been used to greet one another. Then there's the joyful handshake in appreciation for a gift or a kind gesture.

Growing up the only child—the only daughter—of an Army Drill Sergeant, the handshake meant everything. That's not to say you disrespected the salute, but shaking your superior's hand fell in line with the importance of the salute. It only stands to reason that I've always been a big believer in the handshake.

As we've entered the world (might I even offer twilight

zone) of COVID-19, the handshake is now considered taboo. I don't know about anyone else, but that makes me sad. I get it. I just don't have to like it. Many things have changed. The handshake is at the top of the list of things we don't do anymore. Some are even saying they'll never shake hands with anyone ever again. Some are saying they may fist bump. Some say they might elbow bump. Others say they will simply nod or wave. I can hear my daddy turning over in his grave. It makes me almost glad he's not here to witness it.

Certainly, there are many more things COVID-19 has devoured which probably seem more important than the handshake. Our freedoms, for one. But that's a story for another time. It's made us paranoid about almost everything. Leery of our fellow man. Afraid to get close. Much to the delight of germaphobes, it's made us want to be them. I fear, however, it's done much deeper damage than that. It's turned many of us into islands, and that's true sadness in my mind. It's hard to connect at all if you're sitting on an island.

John Donne, the English poet, lived in the late 1500s. He wrote about allowing yourself to become an island. He wrote, it's said, "No man is an island, entire of itself; every man is a piece of the continent, a part of the main." As humans, we feed on the interaction with others. Even The Everly Brothers got in on the idea of living like an island in their song "Lonely Island."

As we get further and further apart, secluding ourselves in our homes, being afraid to get close as we stay six feet apart, will we ever long for the touch of others—the simple handshake? I know I do. My arms ache to hold my grandkids. To hug my daughters. To put my arm around my friends. From the beginning of time, God knew man should not be alone. It's just not good. I miss mingling. Never giving a thought of walking around or walking into a building. The carefree feeling of simply being among others.

I wonder if, at some point in my life, I'll look back to the days of 2020 and realize that's when it happened—during those days. And I'll remember that exact day.

The day the handshake died.

Story #22

There Ain't Enough Rice to Cover Up the Catfish!

And If You Burn the Thanksgiving Turkey Don't Try to Cover That Up Either!

I'M MORE THAN CONFIDENT MY AVERSION TO FRIED FISH BEGAN with the Metz family. Lewis and Madre Metz lived next door to my family in 1955. Mr. and Mrs. Metz had three daughters. My family consisted of my parents and me, so from the beginning, I didn't have a chance. All these people loved fried fish and, in particular, fried catfish. I, on the other hand, hated every stinkin' inch of a fish—dead or alive, fried or baked, smoked or almandine. I must admit, however, fried catfish topped my disgusting food list.

I remember vividly the day we moved next door to the Metz family. I was three years old. Now I had known all of my three years of living that my daddy loved to fish. He couldn't get enough of it. The day he discovered Mr. Metz loved it too, I packed a bag and attempted to run away from home. Even at such a young age, I knew fishing = fish = fish fry!

We all soon discovered that not only did Mr. Metz love to fish, he loved to fry fish. To top it off, he loved to fry catfish. More than any of that, he loved to *eat* fried catfish. That man ate hundreds of them in one sitting. Ever look a catfish in the eye? Nasty looking creatures, I tell you. Bottom feeders—with whiskers. They eat dead stuff off the bottom of the lake. Disgusting, to be sure. And why are they called catfish anyway? That's enough to scare off any kid, from my way of thinking.

But for my parents, this situation couldn't have been better. They loved it all, too. They lived for the fishing trips, fish cleanings, and fish fries. Having no say in the matter, I had to endure this abuse until we moved away. My entire preschool years were ruined for me forever. I had nightmares of giant catfish sucking the life out of my body, filleting me, coating me with cornmeal, and frying me in a cast-iron skillet over an open flame. This fear and utter distaste for fried fish followed me into my adult years.

Enter my husband. We were not married at the time of this awful happening but were at the point in our relationship where we were talking about marriage. The time came for me to meet his family. I write about this incident in my book *Anyone Seen My Rose-colored Glass?* If you haven't read that book, shame on you. It's a funny story that takes you into the world of rice, catfish, and practical jokes. Along with my efforts to not let one morsel of fried catfish enter my body. It's a coverup of gigantic proportions. I learned that day there just ain't enough rice to cover the catfish.

The Thanksgiving turkey affair is another one of those cover-ups my family doesn't like to revisit. But I must. It happened in the year 1991. We were in the process of moving from Georgia to Texas. The movers had taken all our possessions and put them in storage until we could move into our newly-built home. In the meantime, our girls and I moved in with my parents since my husband had already gone to Texas.

Because we wanted to wait until the girls were out of school for the holidays before traveling to our new state, we spent Thanksgiving at my parents' home. My daddy's health had taken a turn and he did not feel well enough to do the turkey. So my husband volunteered. He decided he would smoke the turkey overnight on my daddy's old and unstable grill. Bad move. With the turkey all prepped and ready to cook, he placed it on the grill to slow cook/smoke overnight. But he forgot one teeny-weeny thing. He didn't open the vents.

The next morning, we awoke to find the turkey charcoaled down to the bone. Did you know that stores are (or were in 1991) closed on Thanksgiving Day? There were fifteen people due to arrive at my parents' house later that day. My husband and our son-in-law scoured the city in search of an opened store. Three hours later, they arrived with a fully cooked turkey. How they ever found it, I'll never know. At that point, the coverup began. How would we hide the burnt turkey? My daddy, a chef, laughed so hard I thought he'd fall out of his chair.

We finally decided that any attempt to cover up the incident would eventually be exposed. Not by us, mind you, but our children—the blabbermouthed informers. So my husband, the champion prankster, decided rather than covering up the mishap, he'd just turn it into a prank. He decided to put the turkey out as if nothing were wrong with it, then give the carving utensils to his father and ask him to carve the turkey. He instructed our children under no circumstances to laugh.

When my father-in-law stepped up to the turkey, carving utensils in hand, our children's faces had turned blood red as they tried with all their might not to laugh. Graciousness is all I attribute to the character of my father-in-law as he bowed his head and said, "We thank you, Father, for this delicious food we are about to eat. We thank you for the cooks who worked so hard to prepare it. Be with us this day of Thanksgiving as we gather together as a family to celebrate our blessings and Your love for us. Amen."

By this time our kids could hold it in no longer and burst into laughter. My husband just stood perfectly still mouth agape. When I looked at my father-in-law, he gave me a wink and I knew that he knew. The prank ended up being better than a cover-up.

History speaks to all sorts of cover-ups, whether centered around incompetence, immorality, or crimes. In my lifetime alone, the number of cover-ups I've witnessed is beyond my comprehension or countability.

Even within the Bible there are numerous cover-ups. 2 Samuel 11 tells the story of one of the greatest cover-ups of all time. It involves adultery and murder. The cast of characters includes King David, Bathsheba, Uriah, and Joab. King David gets Bathsheba pregnant while she is married to Uriah. To cover his tracks, he commissions Joab to have Uriah killed in battle. The storyline rivals any soap opera.

The word cover-up, by definition, is an effort to prevent exposure. Most of us know there aren't many things we do in this life, whether good or bad, that someone doesn't find out about. I guess when we're caught up in trying to create a cover-up, we forget we can never hide anything from God, no matter how hard we try. We keep running out of rice to cover up the catfish.

Fifty-seven years have passed since the Metz family came into my life and brought with them the days of fried catfish. Forty-four years have passed since my own personal fried catfish cover-up. Twenty-nine years have passed since the turkey burning cover-up turned prank. Through it all, I've learned a lot, especially about our need to hide our sins and cover up our wrongdoings. In my own life, some lessons learned were hard and some lessons learned were easy. But when it came

If the Story Fits Tell It

to the lesson learned about fried fish—well, I learned there just ain't enough rice to cover up the catfish. And as it pertains to turkeys, if you burn the Thanksgiving turkey don't try to cover it up! One thing's for sure. I'll never forget our dear friends, The Metz Family and I'll never forget the Thanksgiving turkey of 1991.

Story #23

The Unmasking of the Masks

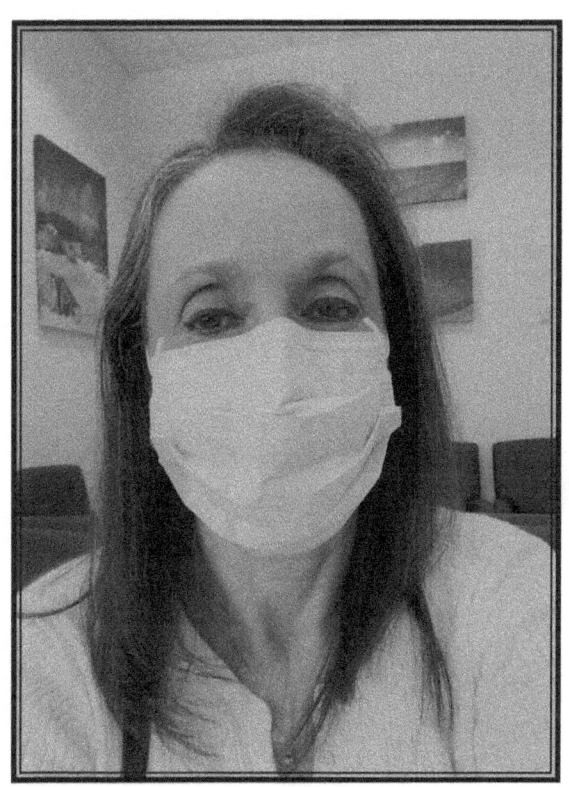

MASKS! DO YOU WEAR 'EM? DO YOU NOT WEAR 'EM? USED TO be (not too long ago, pre COVID-19) if you looked up the word *mask* on your search engine you'd get info about the kind of masks we always thought of when we heard the word mask. You know the ones—superhero masks, masquerade masks, party masks, phantom masks, Halloween masks—remember? Now, post COVID-19, you get masks as it pertains to the virus on the entire first, second, third, fourth.... and so on pages. Have we gone mad?

Look at what we've learned recently about masks. N-95 respirator masks, surgical masks, homemade cloth face masks all to prevent us from catching COVID-19, we're told. There are videos on how to make a mask. And not just one or two. Thousands of them. Again, have we gone mad?

Years ago, I found a poem by Charles C. Finn written in September of 1966. The poem is entitled "Please Hear What I'm Not Saying." It struck a chord then, and I've always remembered it. It's not a poem about the mask-wearing we find ourselves involved in at present. Or is it? There's another poem by Paul Laurence Dunbar (1872-1906), one of the first African American poets to gain national recognition, entitled "We Wear the Mask." These poems address pain, deceit, discrimination, suffering, racism, mental health issues, loneliness, self-worth, and heartache.

Each poem speaks to how people wear masks to hide their feelings or who they really are. The masks they speak of are not real masks; they are simply metaphors for the real meaning of the mask. I suspect many never remove their mask for fear of being discovered. Sad.

Masks have been around for eons. They've been used for

all sorts of manner—for protection, entertainment, disguise, and in performances on stage and screen. We see all sorts of masks during Mardi Gras in New Orleans. My heritage, the Cherokee, made wooden masks and used them as ceremonial masks. So masks have been around a long time.

As a child, I marveled at the masked men I knew. The Lone Ranger, so mysterious with his mask that covered his eyes and nose leaving only his mouth visible. Zorro! Swift with the sword. Both heroes who never wanted their true identities known. Then it got creepy with the likes of Michael Myers from the movie *Halloween* and Jason Voorhees from the *Friday the Thirteenth* movies. Not masks I ever want to encounter.

I recently watched the movie *Joker*. If you're at all familiar with Batman and all the movies surrounding that character, you know the Joker. An evil villain who tried the patience of Batman and wreaked havoc on Gotham City. The movie *Joker* gives the background of how the Joker came to be in the Batman movies. He didn't wear an actual mask, but the mask was there. He merely painted it onto his face, preventing his identity from being revealed. The abuse that led to mental illness that led to the Joker told the viewer of the power of the mask.

It appears masks run the gamut from entertainment to destruction. Which brings us back to the masks of 2020. The COVID-19 mandate of the wearing of the masks. Is it a good thing or is it a bad thing? You're gonna have to figure that one out for yourself. What we see is a bubbling up of rage for and against.

Is the mask a tool used by some to brainwash people into thinking COVID-19 is more serious than it is? Or is the mask the protector of innocent lives? Do we wear masks because we care for the safety of others or ourselves? Do we fear it may become a permanent thing in our society? Is it going to fall under the title of the "new normal"—a term I'm beginning to dislike, maybe even fear? I keep looking back to the time when we mingled without fear. Without masks. The ease of winding in, out, and among people or places. Without masks.

What might happen when the unmasking of the masks begins? Think of what we've been able to hide under those masks. Are you ready for it? Are any of us?

Story #24

Third Grade

How did you make it through third grade? Me? Nightmarishly is the only word that comes to mind. Let's face it, third grade is difficult at best. It's bad enough you start getting real letter grades like A-B-C-D-F instead of the "S" for satisfactory or "U" for unsatisfactory.

My third-grade year began on a high note. I couldn't have been more ready for it. There's always talk about who the best teachers are, and I got Mrs. Little. She came highly recommended by several second graders whose brother or sister had Mrs. Little when they were in third grade. So I felt confident going into a new school year.

When I walked into class on that first day, who should I see but my best friend, Lois. The moment we saw one another, we started screaming. You know how girls scream when they see each other. Craziness. We hugged and jumped up and down, so happy we would be spending the entire school year together.

All teachers know that it's never a good idea to put best friends together. Lois and I were both chatterboxes. In the beginning, Mrs. Little didn't know that, but it didn't take her long to figure it out. She separated us so we could no longer hold social events during her teaching time. It worked. But not for long. Soon we were hanging over classmates talking and laughing. Mrs. Little found herself constantly saying, "Girls, please be quiet." Poor lady. It seldom worked.

When Mrs. Little had finally had enough, she sent us both to the principal's office. The principal gave us a stern talking to and then sent us back to class. It shook us up for about a week before we were back to our old antics.

In our school it was said that upon one's fourth visit to

the principal's office, paddling on the behind occurred. On our fourth visit to the principal's office (our school enforced the three strikes and you're out rule), we discovered that this rule really did exist. Yes, I know, corporal punishment. The indecency of it all. I can testify first hand that it works. No letters, please.

After our encounter with the school principal, Lois and I decided it might be to our advantage not to challenge the authority of our teacher any longer. Despite our efforts, we were not able to turn off our chatterboxes. Lois and I spent many hours either in the corner or sitting outside the classroom. At the end of the first semester, Mrs. Little found herself at her wit's end. She told us if we could not control ourselves, she'd have no alternative but to ask the principal to put one of us in another classroom. Needless to say, that pretty much made an impression. Sadly, again, not for long.

When the new semester began, Mrs. Little informed the class that she would not be with us to finish out the school year. She had to have surgery and would not be able to teach until the following school year. We were to have a substitute teacher. Try as we might Lois and I could hardly contain ourselves. Getting around a new teacher, a sub at that, would be a piece of cake. Oh, the mischief we could get into.

We had no idea that the day Mrs. Little told us she'd be gone was her last day. So, the next day when we walked into class, sitting at Mrs. Little's desk was…drumroll please…my mother! My eyes popped out of my head.

"MOM!" I screamed. "Why are you here? What are you doing sitting at Mrs. Little's desk?"

"I'm your substitute teacher for the remainder of the school year," my mother said smiling.

If the Story Fits Tell It

"But mom! Why didn't you tell me? You didn't tell me. Why didn't you tell me?" I seemed to be rambling in shock.

"I wanted it to be a surprise," she said.

Clearly, I was having a nightmare. I knew I'd wake up in just a minute. Wake up! Wake up! No use. It wasn't a dream. I never thought in a million years that my mother would ever be my teacher. I knew she substituted, but *my* class. This had never happened in the three years I'd been in school. I couldn't understand why she hadn't told me. Sinister plans must have been in the works. No mother would do this to their child. Would they?

Much later in life, I found out that my mother and Mrs. Little had indeed conspired to take down the two most annoying kids in that class. Namely, my accomplice Lois and me. Since nothing seemed to work to stop the two of us from disrupting the class, my mother agreed to take the class, knowing that if she came in as the substitute teacher, I'd be less likely to show off. As an added caveat, my mother and Lois' mother were good friends, putting the pressure on Lois to behave as well. The perfect one-two punch!

As the semester journeyed on toward the end of the school year, my behavior improved. Lois and I no longer held chat fests. We no longer jumped out of our seats and ran to the blackboard to express ourselves.

I'm not sure I've ever forgiven my mother for this heinous—although quite effective—act. It's a school year I'll always remember. But I think the part that stands out in my mind most is the lovely "D" my mother gave me in conduct.

Story #25

What's It All About If It Ain't About the Bling?

A FEW YEARS BACK I FELL IN LOVE WITH THE SONG "PRICE Tag." The words spoke to me. At the time I discovered it, the song and video had already been out for two years. Yes, I know, I'm almost always behind the eight ball. Especially when it comes to some R&B songs.

Most of the lyrics are fantastic. The leaving to Mars thing is a bit strange, but the overall message is good. It's a message I know my parents always tried to instill in me. But then they were depression children, which meant you couldn't find bling back then even if you knew the definition of it. Although I had no siblings, possessions were always based on what I needed and not so much what I wanted.

Once the depression ended, America became the land of milk and honey. It went back to being about the money, money, money. The ironic thing is that as I'm writing about this subject the country is going through another horrific time, a time that will be known as the day we all became victims of COVID-19. It's truly a scary time. People are dying. We're *social distancing,* meaning we're either under stay at home orders or shelter at home orders from the government. Words that make me crazy to write, much less to say aloud. We're living through a time when we feel as though our civil liberties are being stripped from us.

Schools, churches, and many businesses stand closed. The unemployment rate has jumped to 4.4% from a 50-year low of 3.5%. Those who can work from home we consider lucky. We're looking at a job loss that's the worst since the depths of what is known as the Great Recession of 2009. So where's the bling in all this? Where's all the money, money, money? Before this happened, before the evil crept in, the bling appeared everywhere. Seriously. Everywhere you looked you saw bling. You saw people making money. People were happy with their life. Some were happier with their lifestyle than they'd ever been. This country had more jobs available than people. The bling put forth a light so bright it hurt the eyes.

Then suddenly disaster hit like nothing this generation has ever seen before. Nothing like *my* generation has ever seen before. My mother told me once that even though she lived during the Great Depression she never felt it or even knew it existed. Nonetheless, her parents knew, and they were frugal people despite the times. Her family owned a farm. They had all the food, eggs, and milk they needed. And theirs was a huge family. My grandfather was also a carpenter, so he had that, too. But the farm sustained them. It met their every need, whether it came in the form of the vegetables they grew or the cattle, hogs, and chickens they raised.

Today, unless you're a farmer or rancher, you know only one thing—the grocery store. Whether it's the well-known mega grocery chains or local small markets, we don't rely on anything else. Certainly not ourselves for produce or other food items. Then there's OMGosh the actual bling. You know the kind of bling I'm talking about, right? All the beauty products, the ensembles, the jewelry, for goodness sakes. What about that? Not to mention the luxuries. In times of recession or depression, the bling—well, it doesn't bling. It goes out like a light. Then what? What have we left if not the bling? We're faced with the *essentials*. What are those?

I love lists. Let's make a list of what, under normal conditions, we consider essentials. Beside the essential, I'll put whether it's considered an essential at this time:

If the Story Fits Tell It

1. Having our hair and nails done. Nope!
2. Going out to eat. Nope!
3. Sending our kids to school. Nope!
4. Going to the park. Nope!
5. Going to the grocery store. Only if you wear a mask and gloves!
6. Going to the doctor. Only via online visits.
7. Going to church. Nope!
8. Throwing a party. Nope!
9. Going to the movies. Nope!
10. Going to the gym. Nope!
11. Going to museums. Nope!
12. Going to the shopping mall. Nope!
13. Going bowling. Nope!
14. Going to sporting and concert venues. Nope!

Freaks you out doesn't it? I don't go out much during normal times. Too many other things going on in my world. Plus, I'm comfortable at home. However, if I get the urge to go out, I want to be able to do that. Confinement will do that to you. It breeds discontent.

Are we to be content with what we have, as Hebrews 13 tells us? What's wrong with reaching for the bling? As a young married woman, I remember competing with the other wives in my circle of friends. We all wanted more bling than the other one. When visiting one another's homes, we'd scope it out to see what we might find new that we hadn't seen before. Then we'd rush out to find one better. Envy ran deep. We had no idea that Proverbs 14 tells us that *envy makes the bones rot*. None of us were content with what we had. The *price tag* meant a lot.

We're told in Matthew not to lay up treasures on earth. Things tend to get moth-eaten or rusty which destroys them. A thief can steal our bling. What would we do then? But it's inevitable. Things don't last forever. Bling doesn't either. Therefore, we need to look at laying up our treasure in heaven where moths, rust, or thieves can't get to it.

Now, what about the bling? What about the money, money, money? What about all the stuff we hold dear? Titus 3:3 tells us that we've all been foolish sometime in our lives. We've allowed ourselves to be led astray. We've been slaves to all sorts of passions and pleasures (and bling). We've spent our time in malice. Envy even. And what has that gotten us? Hated by others. Hating one another. Here's exactly how Titus 3:3 reads: "For we ourselves were once foolish, disobedient, led astray, slaves to various passions and pleasures, passing our days in malice and envy, hated by others and hating one another."

Easter 2020 will have no bling. We won't enter our churches. We won't dine out for Easter lunch. We won't dance about in our new Easter outfit or Easter bonnet. The Easter Bunny may or may not come, as he's most likely in quarantine. The only Easter egg hunt will take place in our backyard with only the people who live in the house. But like my granddaughter, Haylie, says, "It's still gonna be Easter, Mawmaw." Yes, it is my genius. Easter Sunday will most definitely come.

Do you think maybe COVID-19 brought with it the antidote to greed? Will we see things more clearly now? Will we cherish more the simple things and not just the bling? Will we hug our loved ones a little longer? Will we hold our kids a little longer? Will we appreciate one another more? Will we do the things we should have been doing all along? Will we pay more attention to things around us? Will we learn the art of patience? Will we yank off the price tag and realize there is no price to human life?

Maybe, just maybe, we'll realize that God is in control, that He always has a plan, that His love for us is never-ending, and that when we pray and ask Him for help, turning it all over to Him, that we leave it there—in His hands. Imagine that.

Really, what's it all about if it ain't about the bling? It ain't about much, if that's what it's all about. Because let's face it. Bling is nothing more than ostentatious and flashy jewelry. And there's gotta be more than that to this life.

Keep telling stories.

Best wishes and may God truly bless your endeavors as a storyteller.

I'll be seeing you on the storyteller's stage.

Also By
REGINA STONE MATTHEWS

Children's Books

Elizabeth Marie Hutchinson-When I Dream

Dealing with Margaret-Elizabeth Marie Hutchinson-When I Dream

I'm A Detective! Elizabeth Marie Hutchinson-When I Dream

Arnold J. Peppercorn! Why Must You Have Such a Loud Personality?

Tracks in the Snow

Words and Actions (an e-book)

Non-Fiction Short Stories

Anyone Seen My Rose-colored Glasses?

A Place Called Common Sense

God Moves-Overcoming Obstacles (an anthology book)

Learn more about Regina and her books by visiting her website at www.reginamatthews.com.